Samantha Scott : Beauty Queen Killer

Dale Crowell

Published by Trellis Publishing, 2021.

SAMANTHA SCOTT : BEAUTY QUEEN KILLER

First edition. July 5, 2021.

Copyright © 2021 Dale Crowell.

ISBN: 979-8224251148

Written by Dale Crowell.

SAMANTHA SCOTT :

BEAUTY QUEEN AND KILLER

DALE CROWELL

Andrea Claire aka Samantha Scott had was born in 1941 and grew up in New Jersey.

At the age of 15, Andrea claimed that her mother forced her to marry the man who got her pregnant. In Andrea's words, she was raped but according to her mother, the 22-year old man got Andrea drunk and "took advantage." The man was a friend of her sister and reportedly was either set up on a date with her or picked her up from basketball practice.

Known to her friends as "Drea," Andrea would divorce the man after over two volatile years of abuse but the union still produced two children. Armed with only a 9th grade education, Andrea had no skill set and bounced from job to job. She began working as secretary, waitress, escrow worker, model and touring exotic dancer.

CAROUSEL OF MEN

She married again in a union that lasted three days as her new husband didn't want her to bring her children into the marriage (she met him while setting a trap to find out who was stealing her morning newspaper.) Her third marriage was to a Jordanian national who needed a wife in order to stay in the U.S.

"I married for a third time to a young Jordanian student," she said. "He had cousins in countries that he was afraid he'd be forced to fight against. This touched my heart and I figured 'What's the big deal?'"

They divorced after a few years when the student decided to marry his own childhood sweetheart.

She married a fourth time to a "con man" named Dereck who introduced her to his gay lover.

At some point, Andrea did give birth to a third child but put the baby up for adoption in 1961.

ACTING CAREER

In her mid-20s, Andrea got a few acting gigs, landing parts in M*A*S*H, Bewitched and the Russ Meyer T&A classic Beyond the Valley of the Dolls. She would be credited under the name of Samantha

Scott but would also use pseudonyms of Donna Duzzit, Sarah Stunning, and Prudence Smythe.

"She had been a bit player in a lot of TV shows and movies," Riverside County prosecutor James Hawkins said. "She had some beautiful photographs of herself. Facial, bathing suit, different costumes. She was in plays, movies."

Andrea got roles in some late 1960s "nudie cuties" like Horny Hobo, Wild Gypsies, Nude Django and Bad Girls for the Boys. She did manage two get a two episode run as "Betty" in the show Bewitched which would be the high water mark for her in Hollywood.

"She really couldn't make it as an actress," crime author Diane Fanning said. "So she ended up working as a call girl to make money."

Andrea had been thrown off a horse while filming a b-movie. She injured her back and claimed that this forced her into prostitution.

HIGH-PRICED CALL GIRL & DRUGS

"I was finally dating!" she said recalling her decision to become a call-girl. "I had read all Harold Robbins' books to learn about men and a lot of my dreams did come true through with these 'pay dates.'"

According to her probation report, Andrea began using marijuana in her late twenties and used until 1980. She also indulged in barbiturates and morphine based pain medication after she injured her back in the fall of the horse. During her time as a call-girl, she would use cocaine.

MORE MEN

In March of 1980, she married another man after a whirlwind ten-day courtship. The marriage did not last two weeks as her husband went into a jealous rage. Andrea was able to fend him off with a butcher knife, chasing him out of their Los Angeles apartment.

"Andrea was an exceptionally beautiful woman," forensic psychologist Oscar Newsome said. "I mean absolutely beautiful. She knew how to use her body and looks and words to seduce men and get them to do things for her. She was in several relationships and marriages, all short and quick."

DESPERATION TIME

Now in her late 30s, Andrea knew her days as a high-priced call girl would be numbered. She had to meet a "sugar daddy" and fast.

Enter lumber magnate Robert Sand, who at 69 years old was 30 years Andrea's senior.

"Robert Sand had been a lumberman in the northeast," Hawkins said. "He made a fortune there. Retired to Los Angeles. He also had a long standing history with prostitutes."

Sand had been confined to a wheelchair for years. He suffered from multiple sclerosis and was confined to a wheelchair.

Sand had married his first wife Frances in 1939 but they would divorce in 1947. Five years later, they would remarry. She first found out about her husband's proclivities for prostitutes in 1973 which effectively ended their sexual relationship but not the marriage.

"His wife was divorcing him because he had an $800 a week prostitute habit," Fanning said. "And she was just not comfortable with that and she leaves him. So that's how Andrea comes in Bob Sands life."

By December of 1980, Sand had finalized his divorce with Frances. Then he began living with Andrea.

The rich businessman found the sexy former actress and model irresistible. He booked her for repeated engagements as Andrea gave him sex and massages.

"It got to the point where it got so expensive that his accountant recommended that he stopped spending money on her each month and marry her," Hawkins said. "To save money."

"There was the sizable age difference, of course," forensic psychologist Oscar Newsome said. "And the two were introduced by Andrea's 'madam'. So obviously we're not talking the ideal marriage here. It is an arrangement at best."

The madam informed Andrea that Sand sometimes "played rough" but treated the women he sent to her well "in general."

Andrea's fourth divorce became final in December of 1980 and she then moved into Sand's apartment in Westwood where he asked for her hand in marriage. Andrea said "yes" and they moved to a condo at The Springs in Rancho Mirage.

"They lived in a big, gorgeous home," Fanning said. "In a very wealthy area in Rancho Mirage."

"Rancho Mirage is where a lot of political figures, CEOs, and actress and actors retire," Hawkins said. "Its known as the playground of the presidents."

RESPECTABILITY

Sand provided Andrea what she always wanted, respectability and security. They had famous people in their neighborhood like Tammy Faye Baker. So in the beginning, Andrea enjoyed herself.

She wheeled Robert around in his wheelchair as he watched her play golf and tennis. He took her shopping and she would continue to give him therapeutic massages.

"She did have a power over men," Hawkins said. "She had a way about her. She was very sensual. And she would, for lack of a better term, suck you in."

"Andrea Claire was pushing 40 years old," Newsome said. "She had to have seen the writing on the wall when it came to her stripping and call girl days. She wanted the easy life. The rich life. So when she came across Robert Sand she put her best foot forward. Here was a guy, stuck in a wheelchair and had literally money to burn. Most importantly, she knew that he had multiple sclerosis which would only get worse as time went on. She saw him as an opportunity. Marry the old man, wait until he becomes invalid or dies off then enjoy the benefits of his wealth."

CONTROL FREAK

Robert limited Andrea's social life, however. He was a sexual voyeur and made Andrea pose nude for photograph sessions and walk around their condo naked.

"Robert was an old man confined in a wheelchair," Newsome said. "So like most men in that position, he did not want any kind of competition for Andrea. So he kept her confined to the house. They wouldn't go out to eat. He wouldn't let her out, period. She rebelled, of course, but he really want her to be his on-call sex toy."

According to Andrea, Robert liked to spank her with a paddle and masturbated while he watched her have sex with other men. Andrea claimed that Robert became more and more demanding with his requests and fantasies. Every day the envelope was pushed further and further.

"I think her life would drastically change due to a marital contract that we found," Hawkins said. "She agreed to perform sexual services for him. There was a whole list of them. Some of them somewhat perverted. And he would follow her around and photograph her doing everything."

Robert's demands would be increasingly kinky as the months wore on.

"According to Andrea," Fanning said. "Bob got more and more sexually demanding. And the sex that he wanted was more and more sadistic."

MUTUAL ABUSE?

Robert would have complaints of his own, however. He informed his attorney friend that Andrea would routinely berate and insult him as well as leave him alone for long periods as she went off to "play tennis" and that she had a "terrible temper."

"Sand would complain that Andrea would be abusive," Newsome said. "It is unclear whether or not she would initiate the fights with him or she was responding to his own increasing demands. What is clear is that he got more than he bargained for when he married her as he didn't expect her to fight back or display such a temper."

Robert Sand, however, was not going to throw away a Rolls Royce just because it had a few dents in it.

"But he was also compelled to stay with her because she had the most incredible body he'd ever seen," Hawkins said. "And the sex was wonderful."

POISON THE OLD MAN?

With the arrangement becoming more and more intolerable, Andrea contacted a friend and asked him about the effects of Seconal. She said she had already tried to poison Robert and that it didn't work. She also told her tennis partner that her husband would soon die from multiple sclerosis. Her friend said that multiple sclerosis would not kill her husband, Andrea said, "No. He knows he's going to die very soon."

"Andrea had been a sexual plaything all of her life since the age of 15," Newsome said. "She saw Sand as her only way out and yet this was not going to be as easy as she thought. She began to feel resentful at first then it turned into outright hatred. The sexual games that he made her play, paddle boarding, sadomasochism. For even the most hardened prostitute, it all became too much for her."

"That may have been the straw that broke the camel's back," Hawkins said.

Andrea had enough. She wanted a marriage of convenience from a rapidly dying old man. Instead, she got nightly sexual humiliations from wheelchair bound pervert who didn't want a wife. He wanted a sex slave.

"She thought it would be a life of luxury," Hawkins said. "Instead it was a life of somewhat sexual slavery and she just couldn't stand it anymore. Even though Mr. Sand was in a wheelchair I think he was a very demanding person and he exorcised control over her primarily financially."

THE ATTACK

One night in May of 1981 it all came to a head.

Bob Sand laid on the bed, screaming at Andrea to come into the room and perform her sexual duties.

Andrea, however, had something else in mind.

"That's when she attacked him with the knife," Fanning said.

"It was an out of control frenzy," Hawkins said. "Just stabbing over and over and over again. He was stabbed over 27 times and importantly he was stabbed in the heart and severed the aorta."

"The attack was 'overkill' as one psychiatrist at the time described it," Newsome said. "She stabbed the man over twenty-seven times so this was a hate-filled, raging attack of someone who had a high amount of pent-up anger. All the rage and frustration Andrea felt at the humiliation she suffered, hell, maybe all of the rage she suffered for her whole life bubbled to the surface the moment she started stabbing Robert. And she didn't stop there. She picked up a wooden board that she used for exercise and slammed it down on his head so hard that it caused a fracture."

On May 14th, 1981 at 4 o'clock in the morning, security guards at The Springs investigated an alarm coming from the Sands' address. They found the front door open and were soon greeted by an upset Andrea in a black robe. She told the guards that there was a male intruder in the home and he had run out of the sliding glass door in the living room.

She led the guards into the bedroom where they saw the bloodied, nude body of Robert Sand.

Forty-five minutes later, Sheriff's Detective Fred Lastar arrived and the scene was secured. Andrea repeated the story of the intruder and she was allowed to go visit a neighbor.

Investigators would later establish that Sand had been stabbed 27 times and had been hit over the head several times with a 1' x 4' exercise board. There was in fact a trail of blood from the bedroom to the living room's sliding glass door but they found only a single bloodstain on the patio.

There were no footprints on the grass where Andrea said the intruder escaped.

Lastar also found it odd that in the master bathroom above the toilet there was a wet-t-shirt poster of Andrea with her nipples visible under the thin material.

Andrea would tell the Sheriff that she had taken some sleeping pills and had gone to bed early the previous night. She had heard her husband screaming for help and when she investigated she saw one or two men running out of the house.

"She said she heard her husband yelling out," Hawkins said. "She went down the hallway to his bedroom, she saw some stranger in the dark who bumped into her, pushed her out of the way and ran out of the condominium. She went in there to find Robert on the ground."

She looked and saw that Robert was dead. Oddly, she went and washed her clothes when they had gotten bloodied after she tried to help her husband. Even more strangely, Andrea then went back to sleep for two hours before calling security.

"The problem with Andrea's plan was that not only was she a bad actress," Newsome said. "She was a lousy screenwriter. She came up with this half-cocked story of intruders breaking in and stabbing her husband. Sand is a well-to-do retiree. The intruder takes nothing and leaves the buxom actress all alone to sort things through. Right away, the Sheriffs doubted her story. She implored for them to go out looking for the intruder but they found no signs of forced entry. Nothing that would indicate that a stranger had entered their home for the sole purpose of killing a rich old man in a wheelchair."

No weapon was found in the condo but after a re-examination of the place the police found a four-inch kitchen knife under the couch. The autopsy would reveal that the knife was the murder weapon. When this was revealed to Andrea she went and "prayed" and then would declare that she took the knife out of Sand's chest. She claimed she washed both the knife and her clothes.

Laster then asked Andrea if she were willing to take a lie detector test and she refused. At this point, he considered her to be the prime suspect.

The attack on Sand was brutal. The autopsy revealed that the fatal wounds had been to his aorta. He displayed defensive wounds on his arms and wounds which meant that he had been conscious and trying to ward off the attack. The autopsy physician surmised that Sand had been lying down when the attack took place.

PSYCHOTHERAPY

Andrea consulted with her therapist, Dr. Morton Kurland, and he told her to stop talking to the police and get an attorney. He recommended Gary Scherotter, considered the best criminal attorney in Palm Springs.

Andrea heeded his advice despite the fact it was quickly looking like she was a black widow on the prowl for a rich husband to kill.

A TURN FOR THE BIZARRE

On July 23rd, the Indio Sheriff's department received an emergency call from Andrea Sand's residence.

When police arrived they found Andrea nude on the kitchen floor. Her hands and feet were tied behind her and a knife was stuck in her buttocks.

She told the police that she had returned home after a visit to New Jersey. She stated that two men and a woman had tied her up and repeatedly raped her.

During the rape, the intruders informed her that they had murdered her husband and would be back for more.

"The police came into her home," Fanning said. "She was bound hand and foot. And she had a knife sticking out of her buttocks."

"We never found any evidence of the assault," Hawkins said. "We couldn't find any physical evidence on her."

Detective Chris Brown realized that the rope had been tied with slipknots and there was the possibility that Andrea had tied herself up. During an interview with Andrea, Brown stated that he doubted Andrea's story.

"If you don't believe me, why don't you arrest me?" Andrea challenged.

"It's possible you'll be arrested," Brown said. "Based on my past experience, one of three things is going to happen. You'll either kill yourself, kill someone else, or I'll have another call back here for another phony situation."

MORE "ATTACKS"

Andrea began calling the sheriffs on a regular basis, stating that the same intruders came and raped her again.

"She continued to tell us that the intruders returned, kidnapped and sexually assaulted her repeatedly. There were so many incidents."

She also produced numerous threatening letters which she claimed were from the gang of murderers/rapists.

The letters were determined to be fakes as the only fingerprints on the paper belonged to Andrea herself.

"I've been on the bench for fifteen years," Hawkins said. "And I haven't seen any cases as bizarre as this one.

"In all of her alleged attacks," Newsome said. "Andrea was always the victim. There was never any physical evidence or signs of forced entry. These were phantom intruders. She was tested for DNA and they found nothing. So the police knew that they were dealing with someone who was either schizophrenic or making the lamest attempt to throw them off her trail. Amazing that she had so little foresight into what she was doing. Like a bad screenwriter, she had no one to bounce her bizarre ideas off of so she ended up doing a lot of bizarre things that only tightened the noose around her own neck."

FINDING A NEW MAN

True to the pattern of her life, Andrea could not go long without a new man by her side. She would meet Joe Mack Mims at a Christmas party at the Evangelical Free Church. Mims was 56 years old, widowed and a water pump consultant.

Andrea had a neighbor who encouraged her to "find Jesus" and she came into the church of Mims who was a regular attendee of the services there.

Mims became enamored with Andrea and believed her stories about the murder of her ex-husband and the repeated attacks. He went so far as to visit the Deputy D.A. Jim Hawkins and complained that if they knew anything about police work they "would probably have the murderer by now."

Mims then informed Hawkins that he was going to marry Andrea. Hawkins advised Mims against this, stating that they were going to charge her with the murder of Sand.

"Go ahead and charge her," Mims replied. "I'm still going to marry her."

"He became irate," Hawkins said. "He suggested that I spend my time trying to find the intruders that keep returning and assaulting her. And stop harassing her."

"Mims had a classic case of 'Captain Save-A-Ho,'" Newsome said. "Here was this woman who has worked as a call-girl, has two children, has been married five times and he is naïve enough to believe that after listening to a few sermons she is a changed woman. So he becomes her savior, marches down to the police station to intimidate them, marches down to the D. A's office. All the while, Andrea is not saying a word. She has a new man to do her bidding, to plead her case. She's damn good at finding these kind of men. She had been doing it her whole life."

FIRST DEGREE MURDER CHARGES

On March 25th, 1982, Andrea's attorney Gary Scherotter was notified by the D.A.'s office that Andrea would be charged with first degree murder. Scherotter sent her to the court where she posted $100,000 bail and was set free.

The next day, Andrea and Joe Mims were married.

SIXTH TIME IS A CHARM?

Andrea did not want to sell the condo at The Springs until Sand's estate was settled. Mims sold his own home and moved in with Andrea at The Springs.

"He took it upon himself to try and protect her from the return of the intruders who kept kidnapping and assaulting her," Hawkins said.

"Again, the poor guy is smitten by her charms," Newsome said. "Here is a 56-year old man living as an anonymous life as possible. He meets a woman sixteen years his junior. She's stunning, she's posed in Playboy, been in movies and now she is reformed at the church of his choice. He's convinced she's in love with him and is willing to move heaven and earth to make protect that illusion."

MORE BIZARRE STUNTS

Two months later after they were married, however, Mims called the police and informed them that Andrea had been kidnapped. The officers began a search but Andrea returned home on the same day claiming she had been abducted and raped by the same intruders as before.

No physical evidence was found but Mims remained steadfast in his belief that Andrea was telling the truth.

Andrea was able to put on a false front with Mims, appearing to genuinely care about the man as they would engage in social gatherings at church.

But on Halloween of 1982, Andrea convinced Mims that they should take a drive together. They drove along Highway 74 and turned into an isolated dirt road. Andrea threw a bed sheet on the gravel and began to give Mims fellatio.

Mims climaxed into her mouth after which she spit his semen into a tissue. She then told him to roll over on his stomach and she would give him a massage.

"So Joe thinks this is the best thing going," Fanning said

Mims was like putty under her expert hands but then something hit him hard on the back of the head.

He screamed in pain until he was hit again.

Turning around, he saw Andrea holding a hammer, wanting to hit him again. He pushed her off and grabbed her arm, ripping the hammer out of her grip.

"What in the name of God are you doing?" he asked.

"I've got to knock you out so that people will believe I've been raped."

Mims finally saw the light. He knew that she had thought to use the semen in the tissue to provide evidence she had been raped.

"The fact that she tried to kill him (Mims) was a real game changer," Hawkins said. "The evidence that we needed to really go forward on the case."

KNOCKED INTO COMING INTO HIS SENSES

Mims dressed and drove Andrea home before going to the hospital to get his head stitched up.

The next morning, Mims moved out of the condo. He notified authorities of the assault, prompting an attempted murder charge to be added to the first degree case against Andrea.

Mims moved to have his marriage with Andrea annulled. Andrea's bail was then revoked and she went to jail to await the trial.

Andrea's attorney, Gary Scherotter, now believed that she wasn't mentally stable and had the court examine her for competency. Andrea was taken to Riverside General Hospital for observation and tried to commit suicide twice during her stay there by slashing her wrists.

"Her whole world finally came crashing down," Newsome said. "She was completely out of control. A psychologically broken woman with no way out and no answers, she finally broke down and tried to end it all."

MENTALLY COMPETENT

Scherotter would resign as her attorney as the Sand estate had been tied up in litigation and she could no longer afford to pay him. Andrea was appointed a public defender in Charles Stafford who changed Andrea's please from not guilty to not guilty by reason of insanity. His defense lay in the hopes that the jury would believe that Andrea had been driven crazy by the men in her life who abused her and it all came to a blowout when Robert Sand forced her to be the victim in his bizarre, sadomasochistic fantasies.

But the prosecution found a man named Richard Cordine who was a convict serving a twelve year sentence for robbery at a Nevada State Prison. Cordine stated that Andrea had started a pen pal relationship with him in 1977 which continued for years until Joe Mims found out about it and stopped it. Cordine would testify that Andrea called him after the Sand murder and confessed "I stabbed the bastard."

Her prosecutor, Robert Dunn, would call her a "malingerer who would lie to achieve her own end." He dismissed the idea of Andrea killing Sand out of self-defense on the grounds that Robert was a paraplegic.

"She planned Sand's murder to get money from his will," Dunn said. "She received about $150,000 in cash and $100,000 equity in the couple's condominium."

"She stabbed the man twenty-seven times," Newsome said. "This scared the crap out of the jurors. Andrea would take the stand and give the performance of her life by recounting her tales of abuse but in the end, it was those twenty-seven stab wounds that stayed in the mind of the jurors."

After deliberation, a ten-woman, two man jury found Andrea Mims guilty of first degree murder. The judge sentenced her to 26 years to life and sent her to the California Institute for Women in Frontera.

"When the judge read the verdict to her," Fanning said. "She slammed down a box of tissues on the thing (table) and said 'I killed him because he called me a whore!'"

"Manipulation always worked for Andrea," Newsome said. "She knew how to manipulate men all her life. She thought she could manipulate everyone else the same way, cops, jurors, telling them about her tales of abuse and woe and thereby mitigating her own culpability in all the bad things she did.

REMARRIAGE?

Joe Mims tried to jump start his life after Andrea was sentenced but could not seem to get over her. He knew that she had killed Robert Sand but also believed she had been forced to do it as her attorney had claimed. He then heard a radio program discussing PMS and concluded that Andrea had suffered from the condition when she killed her husband and attacked him.

Mims did research on PMS then visited Andrea in prison, telling her of his findings. Andrea requested progesterone from the jailhouse doctor but the physician found no symptoms of PMS. He finally gave in to her demands, however, and the drug seemed to improve her demeanor.

Andrea displayed good behavior in prison. Mims had a renewed hope that he would get a new trial for Andrea on the basis of his PMS theory. He proposed marriage once again and Andrea accepted. He wrote love letters to Andrea such as the one below:

"My Darling Drea,

I promise you a love that will be true, I will always put you first in my life. I will do all I can to meet your every need, while we are apart it will be hard, but our God will bring you home to me. I love you with all my heart,

Your Hubby,

Joe"

On May 13th, 1986, Mims showed up at the prison to marry Andrea. He never made it past the front gate, however, as he began to experience chest pain then collapse. He was transported to to Chino Community Hospital where he was pronounced dead of a heart attack.

After Mims' death, Andrea once again reiterated her story that intruders had killed Robert Sand.

During her prison term she became a prolific artist at the Central California Women's facility and won several awards as well as becoming a Buddhist.

"I'm very proud of my achievements," she said in a prison newsletter. "I've used the past 20 plus years to improve myself, learning to grow in a positive way and also to heal and forgive myself."

Andrea was paroled in 2012 but suffered from ovarian cancer which soon got into her lungs. She would die at the Mesa Verde Convalescent Hospital in Costa Mesa, CA.

"I do understand that she suffered at the hands of men," Hawkins said. "Why she had the relationship problems that she did but I don't think that was ever an excuse to forgive or forget what she did to Robert Sand."

A MONSTER IN THE CHURCH

PAULA HEARST

CHAPTER ONE

It was a cold winter night in November when the Hansen family attended a service at the Jehovah Lutheran Church in St.Paul, Minnesota. It was a "family night" at the church. Ellen Hansen and her two daughters, Cassie and Vanessa had looked forward to the evening at the church. There would be interactive games and stories plus the young girls would be able to see their friends.

Bill, the girl's father, had other business to attend to that night. He watched as his young daughters got into the car with his wife.

"It is etched in my memory," Bill Hansen recalled. "We had supper and the girls got in the car. Ellen was driving. And they were in the garage and Cassie was sitting in the passenger seat. And she (Cassie) was blowing kisses at me through the window. Waving goodbye."

Ellen arrived at the church at around 6:40 p.m for the 7:00 service. They liked to arrive early and socialize with the other church members before the sermon began. The girls proceeded to go to the children's area, located on the lower level of the church. It was their designated place to be as they usually had their Sunday School classes there, they called it the "Kid's Kingdom."

"I have to go to the bathroom," Cassie said to her mother at around 6:50 p.m.

"Okay," Ellen said. "You know where it's at?"

"I'll be right back," Cassie nodded her head.

Ellen watched her daughter leave and returned her attention to Vanessa and her other playmates. A few minutes later, however, Ellen realized that Cassie had not returned to the auditorium area and began to search for her daughter.

"Cassie?" Ellen called out.

She passed the rest of congregants milling into the auditorium. Her eyes scanning for her daughter among the clusters of families filing into the church.

"Cassie!"

"What's wrong?" one of the church staff members asked.

"I can't find my daughter," Ellen said.

The two began searching for the little girl, poking their head in the bathroom stalls and then going through every nook and cranny of the church.

"She's wearing a blue dress," Ellen said, trying to collect her thoughts. "She's blonde. Blue dress. Blue skirt. White blouse.

It started as a casual search. Cassie had probably went somewhere inside the church, got distracted and lost track of time.

"There you are!" would be the words everyone expected to hear.

As the minutes went by, however, this casual search soon turned into full blown panic. All of the staff members and congregants now began searching through the church, going upstairs and down.

"Cassie!"

Her heart pounding out of her chest, Ellen called her husband.

"I got the phone call from Ellen," Bill said. "Saying that Cassie was missing. And my heart stopped and I think I was breathing heavy, you know, just thinking 'oh boy,' because you know your child and you know that she would just not walk away from something like that. Right away, I know something was definitely wrong."

Ellen and the congregation looked throughout the church for Cassie to no avail.

The police arrived and the response was immediate. Cassie's photograph was promptly distributed to every news outlet and street flyers were made on the spot.

The search began and lasted all night.

"We stayed up all night," Ellen said. "People came all night long to help. There were a couple hundred people. Helping us search."

Police did door to door search in the neighborhood, inquiring with folks with a picture of Cassie. Church and neighborhood volunteers rallied right away and a command center was set up at the church.

There was no sign of Cassie.

She had disappeared into thin air.

CHAPTER TWO

The next morning at 11 o'clock, the police found Cassie's body

"Oh no!" one of the congregants screamed as the word was given to the people who had gathered in the church.

"The search has been called off," the officer in charge said solemnly.

In a dumpster, behind an auto repair shop that was three miles from the church, the body of Cassie Hansen had been found.

The members of the church wailed in agony. Some people stood in shock, frozen in grief.

Things like this don't happen here.

"It truly incensed the community," one of the officers on the scene said. "It incensed a lot of police officers. It was as if he seemed to be treating her as a piece of trash."

One of Cassie's leather shoes without the buckles were found a few blocks away from the dumpster while her second shoe was found later nearby.

"The idea of a church is one place you can go and you'd let your daughter go to a restroom," Catherine Lowe, crime reporter said. "That's something you would do. You'd feel a safeness, there are good people all in there together the last thing you would ever expect, and you'd have no reason to expect a stranger to come into a church and abduct a child."

The autopsy on Cassie's body would reveal no sexual penetration but that some type of sexual act had taken place.

Semen found on her dress would reveal that the perpetrator had type O blood. They would also find unusual, foreign hairs.

Cassie had been strangled to death by a two and a half inch belt, the time of death occurring between 8 o'clock and midnight. The young girl had abrasions on her body which indicated that another belt was used to restrain her. The child had been punched in her face, head, ribs and shoulder. She had scratches on her face that were consistent with someone's hand being held over her mouth.

The police did have one vague description of a possible suspect, however.

One of the church congregants reported seeing a Caucasian male, about 50-60 years old, enter the bathroom area on the night of Cassie's disappearance. He had white hair and glasses.

Who was he?

Police went to work, digging up information on any and all sex offenders in the area.

"We had a total of 107 people who had been identified by the community," an officer said. "Or through police investigation of being possible suspects. Of those 107 individuals, 57 of them either lived or worked in the area where the little girl was abducted from."

Police would rounded up these past offenders and the interrogations began.

They quickly got a suspect and then a confession.

From a crazy woman.

"Vondell Quanley," Thomas Poch said. "A woman from Texas who had claimed to have killed Cassie Hansen. And when she came to the attention of St. Paul police and allegedly made a confession it turned out that what she did was read details in the paper and then recite them. She said 'I claim I acted alone.' Well, it was quite obvious that she couldn't generate seminal fluid and that this was a sham and a fraud."

A helpful call did come in, however. Two witnesses claim that they saw an older white male carrying a motionless child near the auto body shop dumpster on the night Cassie disappeared.

Police followed up on this lead as it echoed what the church congregant witnessed near the church bathrooms.

An elderly white man. White hair. Glasses.

Needing more to go on, the St. Paul police contacted the FBI unit.

With their assistance, the FBI helped St. Paul police come up with a behavioral profile of the child murderer.

"The killer is most likely a Caucasian male," the FBI profiler said. "Someone who is considered a loner."

"How do you mean?"

"We're not talking about someone who is the life of the party here. He can blend in. He can be invisible."

"So the people in church wouldn't necessarily notice him right off the bat?"

"Precisely," the profiler said. "This is a guy who doesn't think a whole lot of himself and automatically thinks that everyone around him sees him the same way. No value. So he keeps to himself and lashes out when he can. He probably has a low-level job or is unemployed. Probably has had numerous sex offenses in the past. He likes to frequent parks or schoolyards. You know, the creepy guy standing on the periphery. He's a voyeur. He watches his victims from afar before making his move. He trolls around at night, thinking of himself as some kind of predator. He can hide better at night. It brings out his mood, his compulsion."

"Do you think he's still here?"

"That's the illogical thing. The perp will not leave the area. He is limited in funds and can't move around easy. He feels put upon and justified in his actions. That he's entitled to whatever he wants. So he often takes a souvenir from his victims. A lock of hair. An article of clothing. Anything that marks the moment. His moment of triumph. He may also return to the scene of the crime, feeling the need to talk about it with someone."

CHAPTER THREE

The perp in the case of Cassie Hansen, did just that courtesy of Dorothy Noga.

Noga, a masseuse at the Comfort Center in St. Paul, called in a tip for the police when she became suspicious of one of her clients.

One of her customers, a cab driver named Stuart Knowlton, had been in her massage parlor the day after Cassie's murder.

Noga remembered Knowlton coming into her parlor at 3 a.m in the morning to introduce himself to the staff. He was hunched over, breathing heavy and talked really fast as if he had just been in a sprint.

He handed out business cards to everyone and received a massage from Noga.

"How's that feel?" Noga asked as she kneaded Knowlton's back.

"Great," Stuart said. "But I need a favor."

"What's that?" Noga asked, expecting the usual request for a "special" massage.

"If anyone asks, tell them I was in here last night."

That made Noga suspicious, knowing that Cassie had been murdered the night before.

Stuart Knowlton looked suspicious and fit the profile. He was Caucasian and 56 years old. Single, he worked a low-level job as a taxi driver. He had beady blue eyes set behind thick-set glasses.

Eyes that gave off the thousand yard stare that only a true psychopath can pull off.

He 'looked' the part. But was he the guy?

"I have no urge for any little girls," Knowlton said during police questioning. "I feel sorry for the little girl for her family. But I did not kill her. I didn't even know she was missing until.."

"Is it possible you killed her and forgot?"

"No sir," Knowlton said. "I did not kill her."

"Where were you on the night of the murder?"

"I was on duty driving my taxi cab. Could not have been me."

Noga followed up with police and offered to tape record her conversations with Knowlton.

Police, however, declined her offer as it would have been too dangerous for the masseuse.

The police also did not want to be seen as obtaining information illegally after Knowlton had contacted a lawyer and the lawyer had told him not to talk. Noga decided to override the police order, however. She was a good listener and could always get men to open up to her. She had four kids of her own and wanted to make the safe streets for other families.

She would then have daily phone conversations with Knowlton with same lasting deep into the night. She described him as being "lonely" and that he could not stop talking about Cassie Hansen's murder.

Noga knew that he was the man who did it.

On one occasion, Noga had taken Knowlton out for a drive. They drove past Cassie's church and noticed that Knowlton had become very agitated and wanted to leave.

The nightly phone calls soon became very taxing. Knowlton believed that the two had some kind of romantic connection. Noga was soon putting herself into a corner that she couldn't escape from.

"I would get so depressed talking to him," Noga told the St. Paul Dispatch. "I wanted to give up. I would just sit and cry."

But finally he broke.

Stuart Knowlton confessed to killing Cassie Hansen.

Noga then started taping their conversations and gave the police the tapes. The police encouraged her to keep up the conversations but Knowlton never mentioned his involvement with the murder again. He still talked about the case in a roundabout way but never confessed to the killing again.

The police would catch another break in the case as another person familiar with Knowlton came forward.

Her name was Janice Rettman. She was in charge of St. Paul's Public Housing Office and met Knowlton when he complained that he was about to be evicted from a Roosevelt Homes public housing project. He stated that his wife was leaving him and taking their two children. The welfare payments and food stamps they had been cut off and he had just begun driving a cab. Rettman investigated his claims, however, and discovered that those were not the reasons he was being evicted.

Residents had complained made sexual advances toward young girls in the housing unit.

Knowlton had let two fourteen year old girls into his apartment to play cards. Once inside, he began describing to them where babies came from and began talking about sex, birth control and menstruation. He then asked if they wanted to see his penis. The girls reported the incident to police which then informed the public housing office. Knowlton was then given a warning by the office that if such an incident would occur again he would be evicted.

Knowlton wouldn't heed the warning. He confronted a nine year old girl and told her to take her pants off for him. The girl was so traumatized that she had recurring nightmares of Knowlton.

Knowlton's wife and children were taken to a women's shelter while he lived in an efficiency apartment. He then told Rettman of his sexual preference for children. He revealed he had spent time in a mental hospital in Traverse City, Michigan after he molested a seven year old girl. He alleged that his own father routinely beat and abused him. And he would talk about shoes a lot.

"I can't remember anyone being as chilling as he was," Rettman recalled as she knew that Knowlton frequented the area where Cassie was murdered. As a cab driver, he would be familiar with the ins and outs of the streets there, the back streets and alleys.

She would call to double-check on his housing situation and found him upset and unwilling to talk. He hung up on her but called her back a few days later. Knowlton said that he "was going through hell, was very lonely, and needed someone to talk to and to visit him."

Rettman offered her services to police, stating that she could meet with Knowlton and wear a wire.

Police accepted her offer.

Knowlton would tell Rettman about the child molestation charges from the Roosevelt Homes, his problems with his wife and his inability to hold down a job. He talked about how he converted to Christianity the previous year after being inspired by a Johnny Cash song.

Knowlton would also make reference to his "explosive temper" during their conversation and mistakenly call Rettman "Dorothy" on two occasions.

"Have you been following the news about Cassie Hansen?" Rettman asked.

"Yeah, I have," Knowlton said. "Police came and talked to me about it."

"Really?"

"They want to find out if he and I were together. If he were up there at the time of the Hansen's girls beatings. I don't even remember where I was that night."

The police then knew they had incriminating evidence against Knowlton. The fact that Cassie had been beaten up had not been released to the public.

"That was crucial and that was very critical," Thomas Poch, prosecuting attorney said. "Because no one had revealed to the press, to the media, to anyone, that she'd been beaten. And only the killer could have known that. Meanwhile, we didn't have any witnesses. It was entirely a circumstantial case."

CHAPTER FOUR

Police followed through with Knowlton's claim that he was working on the night that Cassie Hansen was murdered. With the cooperation of the taxi company, they realized that Knowlton had not turned in his log book. The log book was the time and location of all of a taxi driver's pick-ups and drop-offs.

"What happened to your log book?" police asked Knowlton in another interview.

"It was stolen," Knowlton said.

Knowlton's dispatcher, Donald Whalen would state that he tried to radio Knowlton several times during the night of Cassie's disappearance and could not reach him. Knowlton then tried to buy blank trip sheets from a competing cab company on the day Cassie's body was found.

Dorothy Noga decided to ignore police warnings that Knowlton was dangerous. With her poofy brown hair and overly applied black eye-liner, Noga did not fit the profile of a police informant. She did, however, prove to answer the hero's call when needed.

Noga called Knowlton again in the hopes of entrapping him into making incriminating statements.

"So have you been following the news about Cassie?" Noga asked. "The little girl that was murdered."

"She was a hero for us," one of the police officers said. "She told us that during one of these conversations that he admitted to her that he had killed the little girl. That he had, in effect, killed Cassie. Dorothy Noga agreed and wanted to help in the case and stated that she would be willing to talk to him and to tape these conversations. And she did this hours on end."

Knowlton, however, would not repeat what he told Noga on the phone during their earlier conversation.

Noga didn't realize how much danger she had exposed herself to. After getting off the phone with Knowlton, she was about to close her massage parlor that evening and was confronted by a man inside.

The attack was swift. She left up her hands in defense but the knife slashed through. She squirmed to get away but her assailant stabbed her in the back then slashed down her throat.

Noga crumpled to the ground, losing consciousness as she bled out.

Her assailant escaped into the darkness, blood dripping from his knife.

The thirty-two year old Noga was discovered in the parlor and rushed to the hospital.

"I proceeded to the hospital," one of the policemen on duty said. "Her throat had been slit. Her blood pressure was down to zero. They were certain she was going to die."

Noga would recover from her attack, however. She had been slashed in her throat, back and wrist right after she attempted to record Knowlton's confession.

But Noga had no recollection of the attack. She had to be placed under hypnosis in order to remember the specific details.

During hypnosis, Dorothy was able to remember who stabbed her that night.

She remembered the man's face in the darkness.

It was Stuart Knowlton.

"He jammed a knife straight on in my neck," Noga recalled in a television interview. "Then he pulled it out. Then I knew that he had cut me and I turned my head and he said 'I'll teach you not to talk' and he cut it and he slit it (her throat) all the way down."

She remembered that Stuart had confronted her and accused her of going to the police. He then confessed to the crime, giving her all of the specific details. After he confessed, he took out a knife and began chasing her around the sauna until he slashed at her throat and she lost consciousness.

CHAPTER FIVE

Minnesota State law permits testimony obtained from hypnosis, so any testimony from Noga would have been deemed inadmissible.

The police then focused on the science of the crime.

They had a semen sample that was Type O. DNA was still a long way away from acceptance back in the early 1980s but Stuart Knowlton had Type O blood. The police then acquired a hair sample from Knowlton, sending that along with Cassie Hansen's clothing to the FBI forensic laboratory.

The techs then scraped off any loose hairs and fibers from Cassie's clothing. They wanted to match Knowlton's hair sample with anything on Cassie's clothing.

"Hair comparisons are not a means of absolute personal identification," FBI Lab expert Al Robillard said. "Because a hair matches an individual or has the same microscopic characteristics as that individual's hairs, does not absolutely mean that it came from him. The reason for that is hairs are not so unique that they allow you to reach an absolute conclusion. Its possible that two hairs are so alike that they can't be distinguished microscopically could come from two separate individuals."

But Robillard would make a hair discovery on Cassie's dress that he had never seen before.

"What's so unusual in my career, looking at hairs at the FBI laboratory, I have never seen or I have never matched a hair that had this unusual characteristic. A hair disease called pili annulati. Commonly that is referred to as either ringed hair or banded hair. So I thought this was rather significant."

"If you think of looking at a racoon's tail, you actually see bands. And these bands are created because there is a breakdown in that area of the cuticle that begins to separate."

Robillard then took samples of Knowlton's hair and matched from the ones on Cassie's dress. They both had the same condition.

Pili annulati.

"No doubt about it," Robillard said looking back. "Thousands of hairs over the course of my career. I was only to put two hairs, associate a victim to a suspect, not only through the microscopic characteristics but also through a disease of the hair."

The hair was enough to arrest Knowlton for Cassie's murder.

But asthe police were closing in on Knowlton, the taxi cab driver suffered an accident.

He was crossing the street in St. Paul when a motorist ran into him. The suspect was transported to the hospital where surgeons had to amputate his left leg below the knee.

"It just seemed to me that divine intervention was there," one of the police officers said. "And that the children were going to be protected and that he would not be able to grab another child."

CHAPTER SIX

Noga would take the stand during Knowlton's trial and tell jurors of the telephone call before he attacked her.

"He said he was driving his taxi cab in the vicinity of the Jehovah Evangelical Lutheran church when he needed to use the bathroom," Noga said. "It was there I saw Cassie Hansen."

Knowlton then described greeting Cassie outside the bathroom, talking to her about the church services.

"Would you like to play a game?" he asked.

The girl nodded but remained unsure.

Knowlton lured her outside. Cassie began to cry.

He then her into his cab and molested her.

The little girl kept crying so he put his hand over her mouth until she stopped breathing.

He would then take off both of her shoes before placing her into the dumpster. Knowlton had removed the buckle from the shoe and kept it as a souvenir before dumping the shoes in two separate locations.

"Stuart had a shoe fetish," Janice Rettman said. "When he talked about shoes at first, it meant nothing to me. In retrospect, it was probably more significant than I thought."

The unique hair found on Cassie's hair clothing that matched Stuart Knowlton's own hair strand was enough to convince the jury to find him guilty of first degree murder and second degree misconduct.

He was sentenced to life in prison.

"The evidence from the FBI laboratory was absolutely critical and one piece of evidence that was absolutely essential to tying him in and being able to get a conviction of Stuart Knowlton."

Knowlton was given an opportunity to speak after his sentencing and he went on an incoherent ten minute rant.

"As God is my witness," Knowlton rambled on "I swear to you this day, I did not abduct Cassandra Lynn Hansen from the church she was attending. I had no reason to take anyone's life for God had not given me that right. I have had no reason to have any vengeance against Cassandra Lynn Hansen or Dorothy Noga."

Knowlton would die in prison in 2006 after being denied parole in 2001.

After his sentencing, the Hansen family started a foundation called "Save Cassie's Friends." Two hundred books were printed out in Cassie's honor, raising awareness of child abduction.

SEX, MURDER AND A MILLIONAIRE : THE TRUE STORY OF CELESTE BEARD

DARLA PUGH

"She is really in my mind, a really despicable human being." - crime writer Diane Fanning

Millionaire executive Steven Beard woke up screaming.

Experiencing excruciating pain, he reached down and clutched his stomach. He felt the blood on his hands and panicked. His internal organs were oozing outside his belly.

Beard reached over and called for an ambulance. The paramedics worked in vain to stem his bleeding. The seventy-four-year-old writhed in pain but out of the corner of his eye, he saw his wife Celeste enter the room.

"Oh my God," Celeste said. "Steve! What happened?"

The medics pushed the woman back, not wanting her to interfere in his care.

Chaos ensued as his thirty-seven-year-old wife and her two twin daughters entered the room. Police searched around the premise and found a shell on the ground.

Steven Beard had been shot in his stomach.

But by whom?

Was it the wife who strangely was not sleeping in the same bed. The daughters?

Or would it be Tracey Tarlton, a lesbian lover of Celeste?

"They knew Tracey had pulled the trigger," crime writer Diane Fanning said. "But they suspected someone else was involved. But Tracey just wouldn't talk."

Tarlton harbored a secret from the police. She had fallen in love with Beard's wife, Celeste.

But as Tracey would later find out, there was a lot about Celeste that she didn't know about...

CHAPTER ONE

"Celeste Beard had a very rough childhood," Fanning said. "There was a lot of instability, alcoholic abuse in the family and she really had it rough."

The identity of Beard's biological parents has remained a mystery. She was one of four children raised by adoptive parents, Edwin and Nancy Johnson. Celeste would claim that both Edwin and one of her older adoptive brothers would sexually abuse her from age 4 to 12. Nancy, her adoptive mother, was psychologically unstable and be institutionalized on a regular basis.

On one occasion, Celeste's daughter Kristina would record a conversation she had with Celeste in which she talked about her sexual abuse.

"Do you know what it feels like when you're four years old, you aren't even in kindergarten? Do you know what that does to you?"

Celeste has maintained that both adoptive parents physically abused her when she was a child and that she had tried to kill herself during her early teens. At the age of seventeen, she married Craig Bratcher and gave birth to twins, Jennifer, and Kristina. The relationship with Bratcher was a volatile one, filled with physical assaults and restraining orders. The couple would divorce and Beard would lose custody of the twin daughters.

But Celeste could get men to marry her with ease. Easy come, easy go.

She would go on to marry Henry Wolfe, an Air Force mechanic. Once again, the relationship was tempestuous and Celeste would divorce. She would claim later that her own divorce lawyer gave her money to have a boob job done.

She would then move to Arizona and marry a man named Jimmy Martinez. Celeste had a gutter mouth and would spew vulgarities without any kind of filter. She would refer to Martinez' penis as the "BMW" (Big Mexican wiener) but the two would get divorced despite the alleged size of her husband's package.

By the time Celeste reached her mid-thirties, she was desperate for a better life. She worked as a waitress at the Austin Country Club.

"To use an old-fashioned term," Fanning said. "Celeste Beard was a fortune hunter and she was determined to make her way in the world on the back of someone else."

She would meet the wealthy Steven Beard at the Country Club, fawning over the elderly man as he dined with his wife, Elise.

"At the time, Steven was married to Elise," Fanning said. "And from what everyone was saying, they had a wonderful and happy marriage. Then Elise died of cancer and when that happened Celeste knew what she wanted."

She wanted a rich man.

Steven Beard would do.

CHAPTER TWO

Steven Beard was a self-made millionaire. He served in the Navy and went to college at both TCU and SMU. He started his career in radio advertising in Dallas, literally starting at the bottom. By the 1970s, he had graduated to television and in 1981 he had become the general manager of KBVO in Austin, Texas. Four years later, the station would become one of the first affiliates of the now behemoth Fox Network. The station grew by leaps and bounds and Beard would sell his share in the company which completed his fortune.

Celeste targeted the newly widowed Steven for his money. She preyed upon the loneliness and loss of the TV executive and he fell for her charm.

"She paid attention to him," Steven's daughter Becky Beard said. "That's what she needed at the time. That's what he needed the most was for someone to pay attention to him. And he just went hook, line, and sinker."

Three sweeks after his wife died, Steven would take Celeste out on a date.

He took Celeste to Mama Mia's Italian restaurant then they had a nightcap at his mansion. The executive then allowed Celeste to borrow his $50,000 Lexus and drive herself home.

Steven spared no expense in his courtship probably figuring that the he could make up for the age difference between the two of them with money. He courted the thirty-eight years younger woman with an open checkbook which included a $16,000 diamond cocktail ring, a $3,000 wristwatch, and a new SUV.

But Steven's family, specifically his daughter, grew suspicious of Celeste's interest in her father.

"I think it was money," Becky said. "I think Celeste was after his money."

"Celeste was in dire straits," Orange said. "She had nothing but bad luck in life and men but always failed to see her own hand in her circumstance. With Steven, she had an older man who would overlook all of those things. He would be able to use his money to bail Celeste out of her debt, depression and dumb choices."

Steven had enough money to give Celeste a clean slate. Celeste had committed insurance fraud during her time in Arizona with Jimmy Martinez and had a $20,000 restitution bill that Steven ultimately paid for.

He then funded a renewed custody battle for Celeste's twin daughters. She would win the case and become reunited with Jennifer and Kristina. The couple did not inform the teen daughters of their union until later. Celeste would pretend to be Steven's housekeeper until one of her daughters caught the two in a hotel room during the 1993 Super Bowl.

The union did not have the blessing of Steven's family. They all thought she was marrying him for his money. Steven ignored their counsel and decided to marry Celeste. He was smart enough to have a prenuptial agreement drawn out. In the agreement, Celeste would receive over half-million dollars if they divorced but she would receive up to six million upon his death.

CHAPTER THREE

Celeste took immediate advantage of her newly acquired status as Mrs. Steven Beard. She went on a shopping spree after shopping spree, wildly spending money on whatever whims she could dream up.

"She was insane about spending money," Fanning said. "She could have gone a year and a half wearing a different pair of shoes and purse every day and not run out. At one point he gave her one million outright and she went through it in record time, like six months."

A part of the marriage agreement that Celeste didn't like was the fact that she had to play the role of a loving wife. She had no problem putting on appearances anywhere outside the bedroom. But in the bedroom was where the problem lay.

Celeste didn't want to have sex with Steven.

"She married him only for money," Fanning said. "So obviously she didn't find a seventy-five-year-old man attractive. So she really didn't want to be sexually involved with him."

On February 18th, 1995, Steven and Celeste would exchange vows at the Austin Country Club. Their honeymoon night involved a "sex needle" wherein Celeste had to insert a syringe into the base of Steven's penis in order for it to stiffen. She described the practice as "unromantic" and "kind of traumatizing."

In the months that followed, Steven wanted more sex than Celeste could put up with as she would refuse to inject the syringe into his penis. Feeling gypped, Steven would file for divorce four months after the wedding but changed his mind after Celeste came up with the "oral sex solution".

Sunday mornings would be reserved for pleasing Steven sexually, a day she referred to as the "Sunday Suck."

Celeste would do her wifely duties with great reluctance. She told her daughters that there should be no distractions at all during her Sunday morning time with Steven. She wanted to get things over with as fast as she could.

Things were going well for Steven. He was happy to have a hot, younger wife performing sex for him once a week.

That is, he was happy with the happy endings until he started to feel the financial burn.

Steven had given Celeste a $10,000 a month allowance but she thought of that as mere chicken feed. She had three walk-in closets that she lined with hundreds of pair of shoes, each with a purse to match. She would go on $50,000 shopping sprees and lavish her friends with gifts and parties. The couple would also take lavish vacations, on one occasion they visited China for a month where they spent over $100,000.

Steven started his marriage with over twelve million dollars in net worth. After only a year of marriage to Celeste, he was down to a rapidly dwindling eleven million.

Celeste would want more.

Much more.

CHAPTER FOUR

Celeste pressed Steven for even more money. She argued daily that the half-million prenuptial agreement was too low. She pressed Steven for more money and he would not budge. But Celeste would not let the issue go until one day Steven just relented. He wrote Celeste a check for a half-million dollars.

Six months later, Celeste had blown through the money.

Then she wanted more.

At that point, Steven blew up. He threatened to cut off all of her credit cards.

"Celeste told Steven that she was going to kill herself if Steven cut off her money supply," Orange said. "Shopping was like a drug for her. She had to have her daily fix. Just going to a mall to buy a pair of cheap shoes wouldn't do it for her. She had to have it all. Every day."

And now Steven no longer wanted to pay the price.

"She had to buy things in order to feel good," Orange said. "It wouldn't have mattered how much she purchased. It would have never been enough. Nothing would ever have been enough."

The final straw was the Christmas holidays of 1998. Celeste had spent nearly $300,000 dollars over a few weeks. Steven went ballistic and the shit started to hit the fan. Celeste grew more contemptuous of Steven as he questioned her spending. She often referred to him as "the fat bastard" or "the old fool."

"What the hell is that old man still doing alive?" she would cry out.

Celeste would start to act out even more. She would leave the mansion for long stretches and spend time at a weekend home that Steven owned along the river. She would not go there alone as she often entertained her ex-husband, Jimmy Martinez.

Steven would eventually find about her extra-marital trysts and threaten divorce.

This prompted Celeste to threaten suicide as a form of retaliation. She would be sent to a psychiatric facility called St. David.

There she would meet a woman named Tracey Tarlton.

Tracey was a manager at a trendy bookstore called the BookPeople. She was also an unstable mental patient who was looking for a girlfriend. One look at the glamorous Celeste was all it took for Tracey. She had to try her hand at seducing the heterosexual and married woman.

"Tracey was an emotionally unstable woman who had been in and out of hospitals for depression and other disorders for quite some time," Fanning said.

The two hit it off.

Tracey would claim that Celeste was "extremely flirtatious" with her in the beginning. She said that the two first had sex on March 20th, 1999 and that their relationship would continue until the day she would shoot Steven.

The two were not discreet about their romance. A photo of a company get together showed Celeste sitting on her lesbian lover's lap. People at the party would later report seeing the women kissing passionately.

Celeste was not a lesbian but she was willing to engage in a relationship with Tracey in order to get what she wanted. She admitted during an interview with a psychiatrist that she had to drink copious amounts of alcohol in order to prepare herself for sex with Tracey. Her daughters began seeing books about lesbian love around the house.

But while Celeste had to numb herself with alcohol, Tracey needed no such aids.

She was immediately smitten by Celeste and wrote her love letters just weeks after they met.

"Celeste, you are so beautiful," Tracey wrote. "I think about your long, silky body and your incredible, long legs and I just can't stand it. And then I think of your incredible face and I want to...stand outside your building and wait until I get arrested. We won't even talk about what happens when I think about your sweet, tough, sexy voice."

"Celeste had no problem trading sex for favors," Orange said. "So she used her sexuality in order to get Tracey to do her bidding."

And that bidding would be murder.

CHAPTER FIVE

When Celeste returned home, she could no longer hide her contempt for her husband. She would drug his drinks and then sneak out of the home to party with Tracey.

She couldn't just divorce the millionaire, however, as she had signed a pre-nuptial agreement.

"Because Celeste had signed a pre-nuptial agreement," Fanning said. "She was only guaranteed a minimum amount of money if she divorced Steven and he'd already given her that money and she'd blown it."

Celeste's daughters would catch their mother in bed with Tracey on occasion. Steven, always a step behind, would find out about Tracey just like he found out about Martinez. He would catch them sharing a lesbian kiss on the lips and would promptly chase Tracey out of the house.

Tracey feared for the future of their relationship after it became out in the open. She was in love with Celeste and fantasized about sharing a life together.

Celeste knew this and decided to use Tracey as a pawn.

Going into her best drama queen act, she tearfully told Tracey about how Steven would verbally abuse her on a daily basis. His constant belittling would leave her feeling suicidal.

"What are we going to do?" Tracey asked.

"I don't know," Celeste said. "Maybe we could kill him?"

"We?"

The idle talk soon turned serious as Tracey would do anything to keep Celeste in her life. Both women sat down and began discussing various ways of murdering Steven.

Their first idea was using a homemade botulism technique. They set some food aside, allowing it to spoil and rot. The two women then ground up the presumably poisonous substance and sprinkled it on a chili dog that the served to Steven.

Both of them watched in eager anticipation as Steven placed tainted food into his mouth.

"Jesus," Steven said as he munched on the hot dog. "This is delicious!"

After that attempt didn't so much as produce a tummy ache, the two women spiked Steven's Vodka with 190-proof alcohol (everclear).

The old man passed out and then they fastened a plastic bag around his head. The bag did not have the effect they wanted as he breathed just fine as he slept off the alcohol.

Feeling desperate, they decide to sprinkle grounded up sleeping pills and ecstasy tablets over his steak.

"Wow," Steven said as he chewed on the tender steak. "This is delicious!"

Nothing worked and the two inept killers became more desperate.

Celeste went into her drama queen act again. She told Tracey that she was dreading an upcoming trip to Europe.

"He's going to make me sleep with him," Celeste said in tearful disgust. "I just can't take it. I can't take it anymore."

"I want to help," Tracey said.

"Then do something!"

"Like what?"

"Kill him," Celeste said. "Kill him for me"

CHAPTER SIX

Tracey was willing to do anything for her lover. Celeste came over to her place and Tracey showed off her 20-gauge shotgun. Her father had given it to her as a gift and had her name engraved on the bottom.

"We can use this," Tracey said as Celeste looked the gun over in fake admiration.

"Tracey was there to do the bidding of Celeste," Orange said. "Celeste had all of the power in the relationship."

"Celeste planned the killing out very carefully," Fanning said. "She drugged her husband's drink to make sure he fell asleep. She went into the other wing of the house where she could justifiably say she heard nothing. Then she left the doors open so that Tracey could sneak in."

Tracey was more than a willing accomplice. She believed that once Steve was eliminated, she and Celeste could finally be together.

On October 2nd, 1999 Tracey stepped into the bedroom of the Beard home and shot Steven in his stomach.

"I had stepped into a space that was just numb when I went into that bedroom," Tracey recalled. "And I shot him."

Steven looked over and saw that his guts were literally, outside his stomach.

"911, what's your emergency?"

"I need an ambulance," Steven said in a pained voice. "Hurry."

"What's the emergency?"

"My guts just jumped out of my stomach. They blew out. Yeah, they blew out of my stomach. They're lying on my stomach."

"OK, they're lying on your stomach?"

"Yes, I'm in bed. I'm in awful pain. I'm having a hard time figuring out what happened. I don't know what happened. I've never had this happen before."

Steven was shell-shocked. He had slept through the gunshot but awakened to find himself with a hole in his stomach.

Deputy Alan Howard was the first to arrive at the Beard estate. He rang the doorbell and banged on the front door but received no answer.

Heard headed around toward the side window and saw Steven writhing in pain on the bed. He busted through the sliding glass and entered.

Sgt. Gregory Truitt arrived as well and the two officers thought that Steven had a surgical incision of some sort ripped open.

Two women then entered the bedroom, Celeste, and her daughter Kristina. A few minutes later, a deputy found a shotgun shell near the bed.

The medical emergency now had become a designated crime scene.

Police searched the home and found the bathroom ransacked. But they realized that the drawers that were ransacked "looked too deliberate."

"This wasn't a burglary gone bad," one of the deputies said. "It was a murder attempt staged to look like a break-in."

CHAPTER SEVEN

Tracey had performed the shooting in the belief that Celeste would do her part. Part of her job was to remove any and all evidence that

Tracey was even there, one of which involved removing any shell casings.

But Celeste never picked up the shotgun shell.

She did keep quiet when the investigation ensued. Every family member and friend pointed to Tracey as a possible suspect except Celeste.

Police arrived at Tracey's home and asked if she had a gun. The woman agreed and the police requested that they test the rifle.

A ballistics match was made and Tracey would be arrested.

Steven would not die immediately from the gunshot wound.

His condition stabilized after seven surgeries. He would die four days after being released from the hospital as the wound become infected.

Celeste would remain by his side throughout his prolonged hospital stay.

But she also found time to shop, spending an astonishing $660,000 from October 1999 to March of 2000.

Steven would succumb from the wounds in January of 2000. Tracey Tarlton would be tried and convicted to life in prison for his murder.

True to her word, Tracey would remain silent in regards to Celeste's involvement.

But the police kept after her. They would try to reason with Tracey at first. When that didn't work, they would resort to taunting tactics.

"She really doesn't care about you," the police interrogator would say. "You're going to do the time for her crime?"

The police wouldn't let go because they knew Celeste was involved. But they needed Tracey's testimony.

"The first mistake Celeste made was that she wasn't in the same bed as Steven," Orange said. "When medics arrived, she came into the room and was clearly not sleeping with her husband. Surely that would raise a few eyebrows with police."

"They kept pressuring Tracey," Fanning said. "Trying to get her to give up Celeste because they knew there was no reason for Tracey to do this completely on her own."

Tracey would remain silent. She would wait in her jail cell for the visit from the love of her life, Celeste Beard.

But Celeste was not going anywhere near Tracey's cell.

She now had Steven's money. She didn't need anything else.

CHAPTER EIGHT

Celeste would eventually contact Tracey again. She would go into her drama queen act again, only this time the play acting would force Tracey's hand to break up with her.

Celeste then believed she had gotten away with everything scott free. Her lesbian lover had taken the fall for the murder. She now had carte blanche to Steven's estate, selling off one of the properties for a cool two million.

But like a curse that followed her around throughout her life, all of Celeste's ill-gotten gains would be short lived.

Celeste would marry Cole Johnson, a local bartender, and part-time musician she would meet in a bar in Aspen, Colorado.

Problem was that Tracey would find out about the union.

"Tracey became enraged when she read the marriage announcement," Orange said. "Here she was taking the fall for someone that she believed had loved her. Now this woman was off to a honeymoon in Aspen, Colorado. At that point, she had to realize that Steven was the victim and not her. She must have felt a sinking in her stomach at the realization that she was being played for so long."

Tracey informed the warden that she was ready to talk. She would tell the police the full story of what happened that night in Austin.

CHAPTER NINE

Nearly a year after orchestrating her husband's murder, Celeste Beard would be brought to trial and found guilty of first-degree murder.

"It was wonderful," Steven's daughter, Becky Beard said after Celeste's guilty verdict was announced. "It was absolutely wonderful. It was 'thank you, Lord.'"

"What brought Celeste down was greed," Fanning said. "Self-centeredness. And a willingness to do anything she wanted no matter who stood in the way."

"celeste had initially arrived at Steven's estate with one box of all of her possessions," Orange said. "Steven, in turn, gave her a lake house, a mansion, diamond jewelry, and allowed her to no longer have to work for a living. And how did she repay him? She killed his ass."

Steven Beard's family was allowed to address Celeste during sentencing. His son, Steven, told Celeste to go burn in hell.

But Celeste's own daughter turned on her.

"You say we turned on you," Kristina said. "Well, you turned on us. You turned on the whole Beard family. He let you into his home, loved you, honored, obeyed you, and you violated him and murdered him...Shame on you!"

Celeste will not be eligible for parole until the age of 80. She did not receive the six million "owed" to her after Steven's death. The proceeds of the Beard estate went toward his own children but also to Celeste's daughters, whom he had adopted.

Celeste continues to deny her involvement and now blames her incarceration on her daughters.

"They had two million reasons to lie," she said from her jail cell.

SHEILA LABARRE

PROLOGUE

The farmhouse and surrounding area looked like something from the set of "Little House on the Prairie."

The house on Harvey Farm stood nestled in between tall pine trees, peaceful streams, and wildlife.

A place where you don't expect to find scenes that would be given an "X" rating if it were a horror movie.

The police arrived at the home while conducting a search for a missing young man named Kenneth Countje. They did not have to search far to find evidence of criminal activity. In the front of the property, lay a mattress burning alongside a smoking garbage barrel.

Their first inclination was to believe that the resident was burning garbage. A citation was due, maybe, but they had more pressing matters to attend to.

But upon closer inspection of the barrel, the officers saw a bone sticking out of the garbage.

A femur?

A mass of fleshy goo remained at the knob of the bone and the smell of the charred remains made the policemen gag.

They both gave each other a look of horror. Here in a town where the most serious crime would be a speeding ticket or jaywalking, the police were about to enter a whole world of horror beyond their wildest imagination.

CHAPTER ONE

Epping, New Hampshire.

Population = less than six thousand.

Epping is a rainy, small town that has been sarcastically nicknamed "The Center of the Universe". That has not stopped the residents from hosting parades, canoe races and music festivals. But when Sheila LaBarre arrived, the tiny hamlet soon became known for murder.

"She was a smart woman," forensic psychologist Paula Orange said. "Not book smart but intuitive. She could read people."

Sheila was born Sheila Kaye Bailey in Fort Payne, Alabama in 1958.

She was the youngest of six children. Her first marriage with a man named Ronnie Jennings would last less than two months. Jennings would find out that Sheila had been locking his child from a previous marriage in a closet to punish her. Jennings would divorce Sheila but she would find herself a new man in short order, tying the knot with John Baxter and moving to Chattanooga, Tennessee. Even though married, she would secretly fantasize about being swept away by a rich man. Sheila's mental illness would come to bear in her second marriage and that would end in divorce as well. Despondent, Sheila tried to kill herself and was sent to a psychiatric facility. She would be raped by an orderly inside the hospital.

Now single in Tennessee, the cash-strapped Sheila was forced to live in a local YMCA. She attended a church service and had a private talk with one of the preachers as she wanted "spiritual guidance." She would later claim that the reverend asked if she wanted to "sit in his lap." She then went to a psychiatrist who asked her if she had anal sex with any of her former husbands. The doctor then called Sheila at home and asked if "what she was wearing" and if she "was touching herself."

"If what we are to believe all of Sheila's stories," Orange said. "Then literally all of her interactions with men have ended with them as the pervert and her as the victim. Her sister would later testify that Sheila was molested by her father when she was young. Then her abusive marriages, the rape at the psych facility segues into a spiritual search where she meets a preacher who shows her the tent in his pants. Crazy."

CHAPTER TWO

Sheila turned to personal ads after her failures in marriage. She didn't like the normal courtship process of going to bars and meeting men there. She used the personal ads to cherry pick the men she wanted, men she could dominate.

"Whether on-line or off-line, Sheila behaved like a woman who was in complete control," Orange said. "She would develop a strange kind of power over men. It was almost as if she knew which men would be vulnerable to her feminine wiles and which ones would fight back. But when it came to Dr. Bill LaBarre, it was more of a case of getting the money."

While in Tennessee, Dr. LaBarre decided to take out a personal ad. He would get a response from Sheila who immediately sought to separate herself from the other paramours of the rich doctor.

She sent the doctor nude Polaroids of herself.

The strategy worked.

"She showed no shame in flirting with the older man and soon had him in the palm of her hand," Orange said. "He'd buy her fancy clothes, necklaces, the whole nine yards."

Wilfred "Bill" LaBarre was a successful chiropractor but lonely. Overweight and bespectacled, he had little to offer aside from his wealth. He was in his sixties and recently widowed.

Dr. Labarre was considered a good man by all who knew him. He had been the "Chiropractor of the Year" in 1983 but that would be the same year his beloved Edwina would pass away from cancer. Eager to salve the loneliness, he married another woman named Leona but she abandoned the doctor after a few years. He had two children from his first marriage; Laura and Gregory.

Now alone and widowed, the doctor wanted to spend his golden years enjoying his wealth.

And a young woman.

He would look at the nude Polaroids of the curvaceous Southern Belle, becoming obsessed.

"Here was a lonely, older man who all of a sudden had a 27-year old woman sending him nude photos. He thought he hit the jackpot."

Dr. LaBarre soon invited Sheila to come live with him at his farm in Epping, New Hampshire. The farm was a spacious one, a 115-acre horse ranch that according to LaBarre, "needed a female hand."

Sheila would become enamored by life on the farm, at least at first. She "never heard a June bug before" and the isolated country home gave her a peace that she never experienced.

Neighbors were not shocked that Dr. LaBarre took in such a younger woman as his girlfriend. He reportedly had other girlfriends after his wife died. "Sheila ran all the other girls off," one neighbor said.

But Sheila would prove to be a high-maintenance girlfriend. She would drain Dr. LaBarre's finances, making him buy her gifts and prizes which included a brand-new Silver Mercedes.

She also began to interject herself into LaBarre's estate and business dealings.

The farm that LaBarre owned was called the Old Harvey Farm. It was named after the original owners of the property who still lived in the area. But Sheila forced the doctor to change the name, she wanted it called something that reflected her personality.

The Silver Leopard Farm.

Sheila then had a sign made up and had it placed at the entrance.

She was marking her territory.

CHAPTER THREE

Despite the constant gifts and financial prizes, Sylvia proved to be an ungrateful sugar baby. The relationship would turn tempestuous after a few months. Sheila would claim that Dr. LaBarre often referred to himself as an "old fart" and looked the other way when Sheila began to have different men over for sex.

"He just worried about me when I would date far from home. But he was getting old and his heart would stop beating sometimes."

But the couple fought and police were routinely called to the residence to mediate their domestic disputes.

"You would sometimes hear gunshots," Bruce Allen, a LaBarre neighbor said. "You would hear her screaming, 'I'm going to kill you, you mother fucker!'"

Sheila once pulled a gun on the doctor and forced him out of the home. The chiropractor hid behind a boulder as his girlfriend shot at him.

LaBarre's daughter also recalled that she heard Sheila screaming threats at her father. "I'm gonna kill the horses and I'm going to kill you too."

Laura would later remark at how much her father changed after Sheila came into his life. He went from a normal, well-liked member of the community to a meek, submissive man.

"Sheila was all about being an opportunist," Orange said. "She had the ability to read a man, analyzing his weaknesses, size him up and then push the buttons. With LaBarre, she had a lonely man in front of her. He would tolerate anything in order not to lose her at first and then he simply became fearful of his life. These men in this small New England town did not have the wherewithal to deal with a violent sociopath like Sheila."

Sheila didn't stop with the renaming of Old Harvey Home. She soon took over the accounting duties at LaBarre's chiropractic business. She began organizing the practice into a well-oiled machine. She would track down patients who owed the doctor money and file numerous small claims in the Hampton District Court.

Concerned friends would advise him to dump Sheila before it was too late but it became apparent that the doctor either didn't know how or was afraid to. Dr. LaBarre informed neighbor Bruce Allen that he "had to get rid of her" and that he wanted to "send her back to Alabama. Hopefully, she'll stay there."

Her power over Dr. LaBarre increased to the point where he had given her power of attorney. She began rewriting his will, becoming the executor of his estate. The will stated that he was leaving everything to "a very special lady known as Sheila Kaye Jennings LaBarre."

"The will was very carefully redacted from the original," Orange said. "She kept a lot of the parts of the original and used her own typewriter to amend the little detail of where all the assets will go to. She was very astute and covered her tracks very well for someone who was supposedly schizophrenic."

The two would live together (Sheila would move out briefly but claim to be his common-law wife) from 1987 until LaBarre's death in 2000 at the age of 74. The coroner logged his cause of death as heart disease. There were suspicions among those close to the doctor that believe Sheila poisoned him to hasten the process.

"He was pretty old," Orange said. "And according to the autopsy, the heart disease was significant. So Sheila didn't have anything to do with his death despite the suspicions. The killings would come later."

Sheila would inherit the farm, LaBarre's Chiropractor office, two apartments and a rental home.

This was all valued at over two million dollars in assets.

Strangely, Sheila would marry a Jamaican national named Wayne Ennis in August of 1995 while living with Dr. LaBarre. Ennis drove a tour bus around Jamaica and Sheila made sure that when she toured the islands with Dr. LaBarre that they would cross paths with her Jamaican lover. She arranged for Ennis to obtain a visa and took him back to the farm with her. She would later claim that she and the doctor had stopped having sex and that she "had needs" which apparently Ennis took care of. She would later concede to pleasing the doctor sexually, "I'd use my hand," she said afterward.

Ennis would live in the farmhouse for almost a year. He had his own numerous encounters with Sheila which were violent and bizarre. One night, she ordered him to get in the car. The two then drove around the quiet town, Sheila's voice taking on a conspiratorial tone.

"I wish one of those damn horses would just kick him (Dr. LaBarre) in the head," Sheila said. "Kick him in the head and kill his old ass. I've thought about strangling him myself. But now I have a better idea. I want you to kill him."

Ennis was too frightened to say no to Sheila. The two would eventually divorce and the court records reveal that Sheila took out a restraining order against him.

Ennis disputed the allegations and stated that Sheila was the abuser.

He would later recall being punched, pushed, and shot at by Sheila.

"She told me that she was going to send me back to Jamaica in a box," Ennis said.

Dr. LaBarre told Ennis that Sheila was crazy and believed that she would eventually kill him. He gave the Jamaican money and sent him to the bus station, requesting that he leave town for his own safety.

After the relationship with Ennis ended, Sheila began dating James Brackett.

She and James would remain together for six years despite the fact that Sheila would attack Brackett with a pair of scissors, a machete, and an ax. When all of that failed she tried to shoot him.

The two would break up after which Brackett would get himself a vanity license plate that read "I'm Alive."

Brackett recalled moments where Sheila would act sweet and nice only to go into a violent rage moments later. He said that the greatest example was a time when he was taking a long bath with Sheila only to have her get out of the tub and smash him in the face with a two-foot grill brush.

Two of his teeth would be knocked out from the impact.

Sheila would attack Brackett for a variety of transgressions that would not be guilty of. Hurting her rabbits, damaging her property or having affairs with other women.

Brackett finally had enough, escaping from the farm on one rainy night and hitchhiking back into town.

"I'm lucky to be alive," he would later state.

CHAPTER FOUR

Sheila inherited the farm after LaBarre's death. The doctor's children tried to contest the will but were told that the odds of winning the case were 50/50 at best. They would also have to front over $50,000 to pay for the court costs.

Sheila soon turned the farm into her own private fiefdom. She would hire young men to help her around the place then pay them with her sexual favors or sometimes just beat the shit out of them.

"There would neighbors that would claim to see young men leave her house," Orange said. "They would look beaten up; black eyes, bloody lips, facial contusions. God knows what else."

Her neighbors began to suspect something fishy was going on but had no real evidence to call the police with.

"The first time I met Sheila LaBarre was at the Harvey Farm Stand," said Bonnie Meroth, one of Sheila's neighbors. "It was during the summertime when the produce was ready. I had no basic interaction with her except that of someone standing next to another person as a consumer. And she suddenly turned around and said 'I'll kill you if you come down to my farm' or words to that effect."

Bonnie would later claim that Sheila would try to scare her while driving down the road, nearly running her over while she was on her morning walk.

When she wasn't intimidating neighbors and townsfolk, Sheila would use the farm as the playground for her own private fetishes.

She liked to control and bully men. Stroking one of her pet rabbits, she would punish and insult the men unlucky enough to work at her farm.

"Are you kidding me?" Sheila yelled at the young man who dropped the wheelbarrow. "This should have been done yesterday."

He was young and naive, needing money. If it meant taking lip from Sheila, so be it. He needed work and she seemed nice when she hired him.

"Hurry up!" Sheila said, kicking the man in his buttocks. "Move, move. Are you kidding me? I've never seen a lazier man in my life."

Fatigued after working sixteen hours for seven days straight, the young man keeled over in exhaustion, dropping the wheelbarrow.

"Bitch made, perverted ass pedophile!" Sheila said. "Is this what I am paying you for? I am paying you to work. Now get off your bitch ass. Now!"

It became apparent that Sheila had a gift. A gift of controlling a certain type of man. Verbally abusive and overbearing, she encountered very little resistance.

She kicked the young man again. "Your name is 'bitch', you hear me?"

His real name was Michael Deloge.

CHAPTER FIVE

Deloge had problems as a teen. He got caught up in drugs and found himself on the streets, living out of homeless shelters. In 2004, he would meet Sheila LaBarre.

Deloge became smitten with the woman whom he saw as the life of the party. She would drink beer and play country songs on a guitar. According to Deloge's stepfather, Gordon Boston, the duo would indulge in drugs and study "sadistic material".

Deloge would join Sheila at her farm and soon become her personal whipping boy. Sheila would slap him around like a rag doll. One of the fellow ranch hands, Philip Sullos, recalled witnessing Sheila beating on Deloge with a hardwood stick until he bled. Deloge cowered and took the beating. She would then throw Deloge into a windowless shack and slam the door shut.

Deloge would cower meekly in the corner until Sheila came and got him, making no attempt to escape.

He would be declared missing in 2004 and no one would ever see him again.

In February of 2006, Sheila began looking for a new farmhand. She had her own criteria. He had to be young but pliable to her controlling methods.

She would find the perfect foil in Kenny Countie.

"Kenny was a lovely boy," Carolynn Lodge, Kenny's mother said. "He couldn't do enough for you. Everyone was his friend. I was so proud of him. He never had a horrible word for anybody and that was the problem. He trusted everybody."

Kenny's trust would lead him into Sheila LaBarre's trap.

Kenny would answer one of Sheila's personal ads. The young man was still naive and according to some reports had a "low IQ". The two met through a telephone personal ad service with Sheila calling up the young man and charming him in a way that no woman ever did.

"He (Kenny) told my son Brian that he met a 47-year old woman in New Hampshire," Lodge said. "She owned a farm. She owned a beautiful car. And she was rich. And he was serious about her."

"Kenny fit Sheila's psychological criteria," Orange said. "She targeted men whom she could overpower not only physically but also mentally. She was older than Kenny and light years more cunning. She knows exactly what to say and do to push his buttons. She takes the lead, telling him that he is going to be 'in for the time of his life' and that she 'can't wait to see him.' To a young man with limited experience and intelligence like Kenny, this is music to his ears."

Sheila would arrive at Kenny's home in the silver Mercedes. The silver leopard, the cougar, picking up her prey and taking him back to her lair.

Kenny's family would never see him again.

Sheila would use the same methods on Kenny as she did on the men in the past. She seduced the young man first then isolated him in her farmhouse. Then she berated him verbally before beating the shit out of him with face slaps, punches, and a wooden stick.

The beatings would come to a head during a weekend in February of 2000. Sheila beat Kenny's face into a pulp, took the wooden cane to his legs and may have poisoned him.

Then she decided to take him shopping at Walmart.

Placing him in a wheelchair, she rolled him around the outlet as she stocked up on garden supplies. She dumped two containers of diesel fuel into the prone Kenny's lap.

Little did he know that she would later use the gas to incinerate his body.

Customers gawked at the odd couple, concerned about the contusions on Kenny's face.

"Fuck you looking at?" Sheila would scream as she sped down through the aisle.

Employees of the store soon became concerned, calling the police.

The cops would arrive, confronting the couple in the store. They inquired about Kenny's condition but he didn't respond. Instead, Sheila took the lead, telling Kenny that he "didn't have to talk to these assholes."

The police didn't follow through. Kenny remained silent as Sheila rolled him through the store and out the door. No crime had been witnessed and they let the couple go.

Kenny's mother would later sue the police for negligence but it was tossed out of court in 2010.

A few nights after the Walmart incident, Sheila would make a frantic phone call to the police.

"I got a pervert in my house!" she screamed into the phone. "He's a pedophile! A pedophile!"

In a bizarre sequence of events, Sheila began to play a recording for the detective on the other end. She had routinely audio recorded everything she did, trying to incriminate the young men she worked with into admitting they were pedophiles. On this occasion, she played back a recording of her and Kenny.

"On the tape was my son, vomiting," Lodge said. "He kept saying 'he's faking, he's faking.'"

Sheila would ask Kenny if he was a pedophile on the tape. Kenny would answer 'yes'.

"Now he's a pedophile," Kenny's mother said. "Now he's raping children. Raping his brother. He's vomiting."

The police would write off the call as the rantings of a schizophrenic. They did not immediately respond to the residence.

Sheila would then kill Kenny Countie.

"She had to justify the killing of the young men in her own mind," Orange said. "For some bizarre reason, she would brainwash herself into thinking that her victims were pedophiles. She would repeat the question like a mantra, 'Are you a pedophile? Are you a pedophile?' Working herself up into an angry and violent state of mind before she killed the man."

Sheila's sister, Lynn Noojin, believed that Sheila was sexually abused by her father. Because of this, she became obsessed with child molestation. She would accuse the young men that worked for her of various sexual deviations, including pedophilia, incest, and bestiality.

CHAPTER SIX

After the bizarre call to police, authorities would not arrive at the farmhouse until the next morning. The police would enter the grounds, seeing both the burning mattress and barrel with Kenny's remains. They would not identify the burning bones as belonging to Kenny until much later.

Sheila had murdered Kenny the night before. She attacked Kenny ferociously with a kitchen knife, pushing the already weakened young man to the floor and stabbing away.

Blood sprayed and splattered everywhere.

Sheila then dragged Kenny's body out to her yard where she doused his body with the diesel fuel they had purchased at Walmart.

Lighting a match, she set the dead man on fire. She then took her pet rabbit in her lap, pulled up a chair and watched Kenny Countie burn.

"He was dismembered," Kenny's mother said, fighting tears. "And he was put in a pit and burned. But my son, he just wanted to be loved. I can't imagine what he must have been thinking. Because he was all alone."

Police would look throughout the house and find blood splatter on the walls and floor. A forensic team arrived and matched the blood with Kenny's DNA sample from his Army days. They would find the wallet of Michael Deloge but not his body.

Hundreds of police would spend seventeen days searching the 115-acre property. They found numerous burn pits and blood remains that were so old they had layers of dust on them. They would find clothing that belonged to Deloge and some toes that remain unidentified (it is rumored that the toes may belong to a mysterious Irish man who Sheila claims was stalking her.)

Going on the run from the cops, Sheila hitchhiked along Interstate 293. She was then picked up by Stephen Martello.

"Thanks so much for stopping," Sheila said.

"No problem," Martello said, looking the buxom Southern Belle up and down. His heart began to race.

Will he get lucky?

"My car broke down about two miles back. I got into a fight with my boyfriend and I'm trying to get to Dorchester."

"I'm headed that way," Martello said.

Sheila clutched her purse as if it were a security blanket and she kept looking back at the rear window.

"You all right?" he asked.

"Yeah," Sheila said "Just a little rattled. You know, it has been a tough day."

Martello took Sheila to the drug store when she said she needed to stop off and "buy some things". He tailed Sheila around the store until she bought a douche. Noting her erratic behavior, Martello disappeared out of Sheila's earshot to call the police on his cell phone.

"Hi," Martello said. "Just curious if you folks are looking for someone who just robbed a bank or an escaped mental patient. I just met a woman who is acting kind of strange."

When the authorities informed him that they were not actively investigating someone with that kind of background, Martello took Sheila to a hotel room.

The two would engage in wild and loud sex.

"You just had sex with an angel," Sheila proclaimed after they were done.

"Is that right?"

"You're not like the other men," Sheila said. "My boyfriend, Jesus, I just caught him with a huge stack of child porn. He is a pedophile. So are all those damn cops. Pedophiles, all of them. I think all sex offenders must die."

Martello said nothing. Instead, he put his pants and shoes on as fast as he could as Sheila continued to go on another bizarre rant.

"Vengeance is mine saith the Lord," Sheila said,laying on the bed in post-coital repose. "I was sent back to earth as an angel. I know how to speak to God in Hebrew. Do it every night."

Martello excused himself and high-tailed it out of the hotel room. He arrived home and saw the television broadcast about Sheila. He didn't call the police, worried that he would be an accessory to her crimes. Instead, Martello drove to the station and practically sprinted to the front desk.

"I think I just met Sheila LaBarre."

"To the end, Sheila had control over just about every man put in front of her," Orange said. "Here was a guy who picks her up at the side of the road. He thinks she is crazy enough to where he calls the cops to find out if there are any missing mental patients. He knows that she has a screw loose but he has sex with her anyway. It may be a poor reflection on men for sure but his response is typical. The men that Sheila encountered, from Dr. LaBarre all the way to Stephen Martello, all had the same false narratives going on in their head. They did not see a beautiful woman as something evil. It just didn't fit their narrative. So when Sheila begins her abuse, they just can't believe it. They refuse to hit a 'woman' back. She gets them 'pussy whipped' then beats the shit out of them. Rinse and repeat."

Sheila LaBarre would later be arrested for the murders of Michael Deloge and Kenneth Countje. She would plead no guilty on the grounds of insanity.

"This is a sick, sick woman," her attorney would argue. "Deeply disturbed."

Court-appointed psychiatrists would agree, testifying that Sheila was delusional as well as schizophrenic.

The jury would visit both LaBarre's farm and the Walmart where she frequented first hand. Sheila would join them as well although she was forced to wear a stun belt.

The jury did not buy her insanity defense and found her guilty.

"The fact that she has to remain for the rest of her life behind bars," Kenny's mother said. "She got what she asked for. She'll never see the light of day. Horrible thing is that my son, he's not here with me. He was only twenty-four."

Sheila LaBarre is now serving life in prison without possibility of parole.

THE MISSING BEAUTY QUEEN : THE DISAPPEARANCE OF TARA GRINSTEAD

AMANDA DARLING

"I'm an 11th-grade history teacher at Irwin County High school. I also have a cheerleading squad of Junior Varsity cheerleaders. I just completed my first year of teaching, and I love every bit of it." - Tara Grinstead in a 1999 interview.

Tara Grinstead was a beauty pageant winner and high school teacher who strangely disappeared on October 22nd, 2005.

The mystery of her disappearance is as baffling now as it was over ten years ago. Tara was a beautiful woman in a small town and drew the attention of many men. But as investigators peeled back the onion on her life, they discovered that she had a complex personal life, one with many lovers and layers of relationship any one of whom may have sought to do her harm out of jealousy.

Investigators have pieced together the timeline of her activities prior to her disappearance. But the missing piece lies sometime during the night of October 22nd, 2005, when someone abducted Tara Grinstead and she would never be seen again.

What happened to Tara Grinstead?

EARLY LIFE

Tara was born on November 14th, 1974 to Faye and Billy Grinstead. She grew up in Hawkinsville, Georgia and was a popular cheerleader in high school as well as a diligent student. Her parents would divorce and her father would remarry a woman named Connie to whom Tara grew close to as well.

Tara loved animals, singing and going to church as a kid.

One cannot look upon pictures and video of Tara and not remark that she had a striking beauty. Graced with a voluptuous figure and long black hair, she had the ability to light up any room she walked into. She would eventually compete in beauty pageants, falling in love with the preparation, competition, and glamor of the activity.

"She had been into so many (pageants) that I had lost count," Connie Grinstead said.

Tara meticulously prepared for the pageants, remaining physically fit, taking speech lessons and learning how to sing. She would also graduate from Middle Georgia College and become a teacher at Irwin County High School in Ocilla. She would teach history to 11th graders but not give up on her pageant hopes.

In 1999, she would achieve the first step in her dream to enter the Miss USA contest, when she would win the local title of Miss Tifton.

This victory would allow her to compete in the Miss Georgia pageant. She would also receive scholarship winnings that she would use to help pay for her continuing college education.

"It was, for her, more than a dream come true," Tara's best friend Maria Hulett said. "It was the chance for her to be really proud of herself."

Footage of Tara during the Georgia pageant showed her to be an exuberant woman with a zest for life. She loved to exercise, drink Diet Coke with grenadine, collect Barbies and listening to 80s music like Bon Jovi. She had an infectious smile and played to the camera as she showed off her yellow business suit that she would wear for the pageant interview.

"Why did you pick yellow?" the reporter asked.

"Because it shows that I'm a happy person," Tara said.

With her pageant days behind her, Tara would earn a master's degree in education from Valdosta State University.

"She wanted to be a principal," her friend Oshja Anderson said. "She was well on her way."

Always seeking to improve herself, Tara would teach classes during the day and go to graduate school at night. She also held down a part-time job selling cosmetics at the local department store. By 2005, she had applied for a doctoral program in history and would occasionally fill in as the assistant principal.

"On the surface," forensic psychiatrist Orange said. "Tara's life looked to be a stellar one. She had a bright future in academia and during her pageant days, she learned to put forward the best appearance. But what lurked underneath in her personal life is the mystery."

MARCUS HARPER

At the heart of Tara's disappearance is figuring out the type of relationships she had with the numerous men in her life. She worked as a teacher, went to night school and worked the cosmetics counter at a department store. Outgoing and bubbly, she didn't have the personality type to reject anyone out of hand. She attracted men and had many suitors.

She did have a longtime boyfriend in Marcus Harper.

Harper was an Ocilla police officer who would later become an Army Ranger. Both of Tara's parents liked him as they both expressed the fact that he always remained respectful of them. They have consistently maintained that they never witnessed Harper treating Tara with disrespect.

Tara, however, had expressed to her sister that she was afraid of Marcus.

"She said she was afraid of him," Tara's sister Anita said. "What he had gone through with the Ranger training. He was capable of anything."

"Marcus was a strong Alpha-male type," Orange said. "A cop and an Army Ranger. Tara was rumored to have dated another cop as well but she didn't appear to have a type. From what we can gather, she dated a slew of men from older to younger, and from different walks of life."

About a year prior to her disappearance, Tara had broken up with Marcus. She had given him an ultimatum and wanted to be married. He did not want marriage but wanted to remain committed. The relationship would turn sour at that point.

Tara would begin to date other people. She was in a car with a romantic suitor named Rhett Roberts who was the son of her landlord.

Marcus spotted the couple and would go ballistic, shouting obscenities at Tara.

Despite this angry confrontation, Tara would maintain ties with Marcus. In late July or early August of 2005 they would go to St. Augustine on a beach trip. After their date, Tara would confide to a friend that she was concerned about Marcus's temper.

Marcus would then be deployed back to Iraq a few weeks later. Tara would write the Army Ranger a letter in which she effectively ended their relationship.

According to Marcus, however, their relationship didn't come to a close until October of 2005. He had returned from the Middle East and called Tara to tell her that their relationship was over. Tara was at work and became so distraught that had to pull over to the side of the road. She called a friend who came and took her home. The next day, Tara would call off sick from her teaching job in order to "take a mental health day."

There was a rumor that a cop from a neighboring town, Heath Dykes, came to visit Tara at her school shortly afterward.

"These behaviors certainly show some mental fragilities on the parts of both Tara and Marcus," Orange said. "From what we can gather, it looked like an off-and-on style relationship with a few other romantic partners thrown in for good measure. It is unclear as to who was chasing who at various points of their relationship. If we are to believe Marcus, then she was chasing him. If we are to believe Tara's sister, then she was afraid of him. Why would you chase a man that you were afraid of? Something is not right here."

A few days later, Tara and Marcus would have another "heated argument" which she would tell one of her friends at her night class as well as another friend the next day while she had lunch.

According to Marcus, the argument centered around him breaking up with her. But Tara's sister Anita Gattis had a different story.

"They had a very bad argument," Anita said. "Several days before she went missing, concerning an 18-year-old that he was dating. My sister did not think that (the 18-year-old's) parents would approve of a 30-year-old dating an-18-year-old. I'm told that she threatened to tell the parents and they had a very heated argument over this."

Marcus said the argument was about something else entirely. He stated that she begged him not to end their relationship.

"She wanted me back and all," Marcus said. "And I said, 'I've started shopping outside of Ocilla, I think you need to do the same. Everybody in this town is connected to us one way or another.'"

"She approached me crying," Harper said as he repeated the same story on Greta Van Susteren's TV show. "She was very irrational, and she told me that if she found out I was dating someone, she would commit suicide."

But Tara's friend Osjha disputes the fact that Tara would do or say something like that.

"She's never said anything remotely similar to me ever any time."

Law enforcement authorities don't believe Tara committed suicide as she would have to go to extreme lengths to hide her own body and would have no motive to do so.

"There are a couple of contradictory things at play here," Orange said. "Tara was rumored to have dated some of her students so it would be hypocritical of her to criticize Marcus for dating someone in their teens. And it also doesn't make sense for her to come to Marcus' home begging to get back together. She had her share of suitors, some coming from out of town. She was a beautiful woman and she had options."

To her family's dismay, both the authorities and press would place Tara's life under a microscope. They had discovered that she had "several romantic relationships that occurred in relative proximity to one another."

"There was more rumors and innuendo," Orange said. "There were rumors that she was dating Rhett Roberts, her landlord's son. Rumors that she was dating one of her teenage students. Rumors that she was dating Heath Dyke, a police officer from another county. Even her own brother-in-law, Larry Gattis, was rumored to have an affair with Tara."

Both Larry and Tara's sisters are physicians. Larry specializes in geriatric medicine with only 3.3 out of 5-star reviews on Healthgrades. He was interrogated by investigators and expressed his outrage at the questions they were asking. One question was that if he had an affair with Tara and his response was judged by the polygraph as "deceptive."

ALL THAT AND A STALKER TOO...

Tara would have a stalker in a former student named Anthony Vickers. Friends recalled that Tara had taken special care to tutor Vickers but she later realized that the young man was "unstable."

"He was just kind of a troubled kid and that would be her nature," Osjha said.

Vickers was obsessed with his beauty queen teacher and claimed to have had a romantic relationship with her.

"She talked about the fact that he would call and he would rely on her and she knew it was getting too much for her," a friend named Maria said. "I just kept telling her, 'You know Tara, something's wrong."

Vickers was two years out of high school when he came to Tara's house and demanded to be let in. He pounded on the door until she called the police. Vickers resisted arrest but charges were later dropped and no restraining orders were ever filed.

The Vickers incident wasn't the only occasion that the former beauty pageant winner was being stalked. There was an incident where someone would call her home and make threats. The call was traced and it was determined to be a student in her homeroom who was promptly removed from the class.

THE NIGHT OF...

Before the night of her disappearance, Tara had enjoyed the company of her friend Dana and some teenage girls as they readied for the "Miss Georgia Sweet Potato" pageant. Her friend remembered

Tara as being in a great mood, helping out the girls with their hair and makeup. She would attend the pageant where she served as a backstage coach. Later that evening, she went to the house of a neighbor before going to a barbecue a few blocks from her home . Police believe that she had remained at the barbecue until 11 pm when she left to go home. They would find the clothes she wore at the cookout on her bedroom floor which indicated to police that she had, in fact, returned home.

From that point on, police "have no idea" what happened to Tara.

On October 24th, 2005, Tara did not show up to teach her class. Her colleagues called the police who showed up at her residence to do a welfare check. They would find her white Mitsubishi parked in the garage, unlocked. Upon entering her home, police found a business card lodged in her door.

There appeared to be no sign of forced entry. Searching through the house, police found her cell phone plugged into her charger. Her purse and keys could not be found.

Strangely, the clothes she wore the night before were piled on the bedroom floor.

Investigators found it odd that the car door was unlocked and that the car seat was pushed back. Tara was petite at only five-foot-three and would have kept the seat much closer to the steering wheel. They found an envelope of cash (one hundred dollars) on her dashboard while both her dog and cat were inside. Tara's sister said that she was an animal lover who would never just abandon her pets.

Something was wrong...

The police immediately called the Georgia Bureau of Investigation as the lacked the resources to pursue this kind of crime.

Taking over the case, the GBI believed that Tara may have left with someone that she knew, given the lack of a forced entry and the fact that only her purse and keys were missing. Neighbors did not report hearing any screaming at night.

Her disappearance shocked the small and close-knit community. To a person, Tara was described as someone who had a great personality, loved by faculty and students alike. Nothing in her professional life would suggest that she had any enemies.

Volunteers from the community immediately went to work. Irwin County students, teachers, and other townsfolk searched the area and put out flyers.

"Missing. Tara Grinstead. $20,000 Reward."

ROUNDING UP THE SUSPECTS

Longtime boyfriend Marcus Harper was one of the first to be questioned. He came with a ready-made alibi for the night of Tara's disappearance.

Marcus was seen at a bar with friends then went on a 'ride-along' with a former partner on the local police force. His whereabouts was "essentially substantiated" according to authorities.

Former student/stalker Anthony Vickers was questioned but later ruled out as a suspect. Like the others, however, he could not account for the entire thirty-four hour period when Tara was last seen and reported missing.

"Vickers is probably the only one I would rule out," Orange said. "This disappearance was too clean. Vickers was a disturbed twenty-year-old man with a crush. He would not have the emotional wherewithal or the knowledge to pull off a crime with no clues. But someone with law enforcement or medical training could."

But who left the business card behind at her door?

The card was left by Heath Dykes, a married Perry police officer with two children. He was from the next town over and had known Tara since high school.

Neighbors would tell investigators that he visited Tara's house often. It is unclear what their relationship was (outside of the obvious innuendo and rumors).

Still, he had left close to two dozen messages on Tara's answering message on the weekend she went missing.

There is small-town gossip that the two were having an affair. Local witnesses have confirmed that they saw his wife throw his clothes out on the front lawn. The content of the messages he left have not been made public but the rumors were that he was telling her "he was sorry" and that he "loved her."

What is clear is that he did call Tara's mother from the front yard and ask if she knew where Tara was and if she was alright.

Heath Dykes was the last known person at Tara's home that night as he arrived a little after midnight.

"There are simply too many secrets here," Orange said. "Something was clearly going on in Heath's mind in order for him to call Tara that many times over the course of one evening. One rumor is that they were having an affair and that she was going to tell his wife. So he was calling her in a desperate attempt to stop her from doing that. Another possibility was that she was calling him for help and he was returning her calls. His involvement led to a lot of outlandish speculation, one of which was that Heath knew that a hit man was coming for Tara and that he was calling to make sure that she was okay."

"I think the fact that she was beautiful and other people paid attention to her would obviously make some people jealous," Tara's friend Maria said. "I think she was afraid of the possibility of someone hurting her from being angry at her, having reactions to her dating people."

Numerous men were rounded up and questioned, there was Jim Perry who dated Tara years earlier, Rhett Roberts, Marcus Harper, Anthony Vickers, and Eric Cook among others.

Another unsubstantiated rumor that Tara was involved with another student named Eric Cook. A friend of his had made mention of their affair in an Internet forum post where he stated that everyone knew that they were "messing around." He also said that the police didn't make the information public out of respect for Tara's family as she dated around quite a bit. An alleged friend of Cook disputed the rumor on the forum, however. Cook would later die in a car accident.

A neighbor, Joe Poirier lived with his wife and was rumored to have been "obsessed" with Tara. The older couple admitted to "looking out for Tara" and they were fond of her. He was seen pouring concrete near his home the day after she disappeared.

Another person of interest was Larry Gattis, the brother-in-law of Tara. He was brought in for questioning after the disappearance. It would later be revealed that he had been asked if he had an affair with Tara.

Larry answered 'no'.

The polygraph machine marked it as a 'deceptive answer.'

48 HOURS

In 2008, Tara's case would be featured on the CBS News show "48 Hours Mystery." The show would illustrate the parallels between Tara's case and the disappearance of Jennifer Kesse who would go missing in Orlando, Florida three months later. The GBI would also reveal during the broadcast that they had found a latex glove in Tara's yard just a few feet away from her front porch.

The GBI forensic team would analyze the DNA left in the glove and determine that it was a man's DNA, they just do not know who it belongs to. They would compare the DNA samples of the numerous men who were associated with or knew Tara but none of them have matched.

The DNA has also been entered into the Georgia and national databases but no match has been made to date.

"The glove may be a red herring," Orange said. "Whoever entered the home left nothing behind, no prints, DNA, nothing. So it was obviously someone who knew exactly what they were doing. They wanted to harm Tara."

A HOAX AND FALSE TIPS

In February of 2009, a man calling himself the "Catch Me Killer" began posting videos boasting that he had murdered sixteen women. One of the women he described had a close resemblance to Tara Grinstead. The man producing the video digitally obscured his face and voice but police eventually identified the culprit as twenty-seven-year-old Andrew Haley.

Haley performed the videos as part of a bizarre hoax and was eliminated as a possible suspect.

Investigator Gary Rothwell has expressed his lament at how the rumors and speculation have caused unfair stress to many who have been already tried in the public eye. "Irresponsible public accusations have been made about them, and they have no way to respond or defend themselves. And it's frustrating that we don't have evidence to rule anyone in or out."

Rothwell admits, however, that he has information that has not been released.

In February of 2015, authorities acted on a tip which led them to drain a pond in Fitzgerald, Georgia.

They didn't go into details as to what the specifics of the tip were. The pond would be drained and nothing would be found.

ALIBIS

Police have alibis from all the men who knew Tara Grinstead but no one has been ruled out because no one can account for the full thirty-four hour period.

Rhett Reynolds stated he went to sleep after the cookout. Joe Poirier was with his wife next door.

The most elaborate alibi, however, came from Marcus Harper.

Again, Marcus was in a local bar and a friend of Tara's had spotted him there. She would call Tara at around 10:15 and 10:30 to tell Tara that Marcus was there.

After 1 am, Marcus left the bar and went to look for his police officer friend, Sgt. Sean Fletcher. Fletcher was on duty that night.

Fletcher knew Tara as well. Ironically, he was one of the officers who arrived at Tara's house when Anthony Vickers, Tara's former student, was banging on her door.

There were rumors that Tara didn't like Fletcher because he had told Harper that Tara was entertaining Heath Dykes at her home.

Fletcher would deny that speculation.

"What we can extrapolate from this scenario was that Vickers was angry that his crush, Tara, was with another man," Orange said. "So he goes to her home and demands that she talk to him. He's young, twenty-years-old, and doesn't understand why she would do this to him. He is then arrested by Fletcher who relays what Tara is doing to Marcus, a man that Tara is wary about because of his temper. So now we have more than just a love triangle, it is a love octagon, with numerous men vying for and getting jealous over the attention of Tara."

At around 1:49 am, Fletcher received a call from dispatch informing him that Marcus Harper was looking for him. The two met up and walked Fletcher's beat, checking doors in downtown Ocilla.

Around 2:45, Fletcher was dispatch to a home where a mentally unbalanced man, Bennie Merritt, had stumbled into a home and refused to leave. Marcus would join Fletcher on the call as did two other officers. Merritt, however, was gone from the premises.

Minutes later, they began to search for Merritt who was also a neighbor of Tara's. The drunken Merritt would accost the cashier at the local gas station then be apprehended. Both Fletcher and Harper had responded to the call at the gas station and by the time they were done it was 4:28 am.

Marcus then headed home.

Investigators would later be able to corroborate these details with multiple witnesses, including Merritt, who was scrutinized as a possible suspect in the kidnapping as well.

Marcus Harper, however, has not been ruled out as a potential person of interest in the case.

"Marcus's alibi is too perfect," GBI investigator Maurice Godwin said.

Both Larry and Anita Gattis believe that Marcus is the top suspect.

"He had the motive," Tara's sister said. "And the training."

The insinuation would draw the ire of Marcus who became upset that Anita consistently brought up his military and police training. He continues to deny any involvement in Tara's disappearance.

"I don't wanna hurt any innocent civilian much less someone I spent five and a half years of my life with."

"What is clear is that there isn't a whole lot forthcoming about Tara's personal life to draw the conclusions we need to about who is the most probable suspect," Orange said. "Like in the Natalee Holloway case, the sexual activity of the woman in question is kept hidden. If her background reveals that she was a promiscuous woman, there will e less sympathy and urgency to solve the crime. That is one of the more striking aspects of the case, aside from Tara's vanishing, is the cover-up of Tara's personal life in order to protect her reputation."

UNSOLVABLE CASE?

Tara Grinstead's case is still being investigated. The GBI reports that they receive numerous leads per day, most of which are false.

Her body has never been found but her impact on the lives of those around her and her students will never be forgotten.

"I'm so sorry to hear about what happened to Miss Grinstead," said Christine Kang, a South Korean exchange student from Grinstead's class. "She is so caring and giving to her students. I am sure she will come home soon safely. I will pray for her every night."

MISTY COPSEY

Misty Copsey was fourteen years old when she disappeared on September 17th, 1992 after a trip to the Puyallup Fair.

Her case remains a showcase of administrative screw-ups and dropped balls. She was initially thought of as a runaway before foul play was finally suspected a month after the fact. Subsequently, there have been at least five people suspected of committing her abduction.

But the Puyallup police did not get within sniffing distance of Misty or charging anyone with her disappearance. Three different police chiefs and numerous detectives all took a swing at the case and whiffed. No one in law enforcement has been able to answer the question on everyone's lips.

What happened to Misty Copsey?

A GOOD GIRL

Misty was born in 1978 to Diana and Paul "Buck" Copsey. Her father was a firefighter but the couple split up shortly after she was born and Misty lived with her mother.

Misty got good grades in school, excelling particularly in Math. During her last quarter at Spanaway Lake Junior High School, she got A's and B's. Athletic, she played softball, volleyball, and basketball before breaking both forearms during an athletic practice.

Misty was not the ringleader of a bad crowd. She was diffident but funny, entertaining her friends while skipping around and singing the theme song to Sesame Street.

She did not have much in regards to material wants. Her mother eked out a living as an in-home care nurse and they lived in a mobile home park until she was fourteen. Seeking a better place to live, Diana and Misty moved into a duplex where she now had her own room. But Misty longed for her friend who lived in and around the old trailer park. She would make it back there when she could to just hang out.

Tall, blonde and with green eyes, Misty was cute enough to draw the attention of boys. She remained chaste, however, and was not dating like so many of her other friends.

Her innocent, girl-next-door looks would draw the attention of Rheuban Schmidt. Rheuban looked like a casting call actor for a meth head. He sported a reverse mullet, a hairstyle that was cut close to the sides with curls on top. He had beady, green eyes that screamed low IQ. One of Misty's friends described him as a "scuzzy looking dude" but he nonetheless befriends Misty, much to the chagrin of her mother.

Diana grew suspicious of the relationship as Rheuban was four years older and a high school dropout. On one occasion, she listened in on the other end of a phone conversation Misty was having with Rheuban.

"I get horny just looking at you, Misty," Rheuban said, whispering like an old pervert.

Diana became enraged and ordered her daughter off the phone.

"Don't ever talk to that idiot again...."

ENTER CORY BOBER

Cory Bober was a thorn in the side of police every since the Green River killings became a national news story. He would insist that the police are "incompetent fools" while organizing his own searches for her remains. Diana would later accuse him of killing her daughter but he would respond by telling Diana that she was being "ungrateful." He was, after all, the only man on the case.

Bober was a recluse without a vehicle or a drive's license. An inveterate marijuana user, he had a record for both possession and dealing. He was also obsessed with cases of murdered or slain women in his home state of Washington. He had a stack of binders with autopsy reports, pictures, and other arcane details.

Bober came under the radar of the police in Puyallup when he became obsessed with the Green River Killer case. He had a brief acquaintance with Randall Dean Achziger, remembering a conversation where the man told him that the killer inserted rocks into the remains of his victim. Bober became suspicious as that would turn out to be a piece of information only known to police. He then went on a one-man crusade to prove the guilt of Achziger. Bober would interview his ex-girlfriends, friends, co-workers and present all of this in an affidavit to the courts.

Achziger found it ridiculous and annoying.

So did the police.

The Green River Killer would turn out to be a painter named Gary Leon Ridgway.

Bober didn't give up, however. He knew Achziger was the guy.

Bober had his own theories about who was performing the killings. Some were wild and outlandish conspiracy theories. Others were spot on. He would notice that there were victims that "had disappeared on the very same date that others were discovered. Some victims seemed to almost 'commemorate' the deaths or discoveries of others; one would die on a particular date and another would disappear a year to the day later on the very same date."

The police dismissed his theories as the rantings of a crack head. But Bober would be willing to show the proof of his connect the dots calculations. He pointed to the cases of Kim Delange, a 15-year-old killed in 1988 and Anna Chebetnoy, a 14-year-old killed in 1990. Both of their bodies would be found along Highway 410, east of Enumclaw.

Bober discovered that the remains of both girls were found in the same section of 410. The girls were found two years and one month apart. He felt that the killer was following a pattern.

He called the police department and left a voice mail. He predicted that a teen girl from Puyallup would disappear and her remains would be found on Highway 410 in the same vicinity where the other girl's bodies were found. Bober gave him the name of the man whom he felt was the serial killer.

Randall Achziger.

But the police were now used to his calls and viewed him as a crank. A nutcake with a strange vendetta.

His prediction would be half-right, however.

There would be no body found on Highway 410.

But a teenage girl would disappear.

Her name was Misty Copsey.

A NIGHT AT THE FAIR

On September 17th, 1992, Diana told her daughter Misty and her best friend Trina Bevard to behave themselves. Misty had convinced her mother to let them stay out that night...free of any meddlesome adults. But Trina's guardian would not allow her to go without an adult driving them home.

Diana worked as a caregiver for a 97-year-old Alzheimer patient who could not be left alone. She would not be able to drive the girls home. But Misty checked the bus schedules and convinced her mother that they would be okay. There was a bus that left the fair at 8:40 p.m.

Misty then convinced her mother to lie to Trina's guardian, Marlene Shoemaker.

"No worries," Diana said to Marlene. "I'll bring them home."

She wanted to be the cool parent, different from the stuffy adults who forgot what it was like to be fourteen. If it meant telling a white lie so her little girl could have some happiness, so be it.

What was the worst that could happen?

Diana dropped the girls off and gave them one last warning.

"Get home safe."

It would be the last time she would ever see her daughter again.

THE PHONE CALL

A few hours later, Diana would then receive a phone call from Misty as she tended to her elderly patient. Misty told her that she had missed the bus but could get a ride from Rheuban Schmidt.

Diana, knowing what kind of unsavory character Schmidt was, adamantly refused. She told Misty to find someone else to give her a ride back. Misty had an electronic diary which she used to store phone numbers. She told her mother she would find someone trustworthy to call for a ride.

"You call me back when you find someone," Diana said.

"I will. I promise."

Diana would wait all night for the phone call.

In the ensuing hours, Misty would not call back.

Worried, Diane called home in the hope that Misty had gotten a ride without calling her.

No answer.

Diana didn't panic. She figured that Misty went home with that scumbag Schmidt and didn't want to get yelled out for disobeying her.

She's going to get yelled at either/or. All Diana wanted was for her daughter to be safe.

Her shift finally ended and Diana drove back home in a rush.

Upon entering her house, she called out for Misty.

Silence.

She went into Misty's room and saw that it had been untouched from the previous night.

Diana would call the police in a panic. She told them that her daughter had not come home from the fair. The dispatcher would tell her that the police could not do anything about it for thirty days as it "sounded like a runaway case."

Diana knew otherwise.

Trying to calm herself, she figured that Misty was with Trina, that the two of them would be okay.

She called Trina's home.

No answer.

She then began scorching the earth with phone calls.

She would call Rheuban but he told her that she called but he didn't have the gas to go get her. She then called numerous friends of Misty and her mother.

No one had seen Misty.

She called Trina's home again, got no answer, then drove out to her house. She then went to the police department and filed a formal report with the Pierce County's Sheriff's Department who handled runaways as opposed to the Puyallup Police.

MISTY'S MISSING

Misty's friend Trina called Diana after she came back from school. She told the frantic mother that she didn't know where Misty was.

"The last time I saw her, she was heading for the bus," she said.

Diana would call Rheuban again. She would get his roommate this time, James Tinsley.

Diana needed answers. She interrogated the young fifteen-year-old like a grizzled police detective. She asked if Rheuban had been home all night. James then told her that Rheuban and his uncle went to pick up Misty but that he wasn't home just yet.

Later, Diana would call back and Rheuban would tell her that his roommate got the story wrong. He went to a party instead and didn't pick up Misty. He didn't know where she was.

Diana pleaded for the police to do something. They dragged their heels and began talking to some of Misty's friends. "Just call if she calls," they informed them. "No one gets in trouble."

Diana printed fliers with Misty's picture. She plastered them in and around the fairgrounds while calling the media.

The one woman search team would yield no leads. Rheuban would stop by and ask if the police had found anything yet. Diana would then wait at the bus stop near the fairgrounds to inquire with different drivers on the route. She found one driver who said that he saw Misty. She had asked when the next bus to Spanaway was arriving. The driver said it wasn't and that he was done for the night. He gave her instructions on which bus to take but she walked away before he could complete his sentence.

AN ERROR OF JUDGEMENT

Among the many mistakes that the Puyallup police made in the investigation of Misty's disappearance was to make the assumption that she was a runaway. Why they didn't entertain the prospect that she could have been kidnapped and murdered gave the abductor precious time to cover his tracks.

The police came to this erroneous conclusion after they interviewed Misty's mother, Diana. They thought she was a liar and an alcoholic. They then interviewed a pair of Misty's classmates who really didn't know her that well or accompany her to the fair.

A series of cover-ups then ensued, as the police told the media Misty had been found (where they got that information remains a mystery) and made no further investigation.

Until Diana and the media started to make a fuss. The department had to save face and eventually one of the detectives believed that this was not a runaway case.

Misty's disappearance could not be ignored any longer.

Police would talk to the various fair workers and security guards. No one had recalled seeing Misty.

The police then turned to her family, interviewing and doing background checks on both Misty's father, Buck, and Diana.

Their impressions of the duo would support their initial theory that Misty runaway. Diana was an alcoholic with multiple DUIs and seven years prior she had been convicted of welfare fraud. Buck confirmed that his daughter and Diana would have their issues.

Carver then discovered that Diana had filed a runaway report on Misty a month prior to her disappearing.

Diana would later state that the report was wrong. She thought Misty had disappeared then found her in the bedroom. She was too ashamed to tell the police it had been a false alarm.

With the police questioning and media coverage, Misty Copsey was now the talk of her Spanaway Lake Junior High school.

Rumors would abound at the school, one of which came from Misty Matthews who said that Misty had called her from Olympia. Another student stated that she saw Misty at a Color Me Badd concert at the fair.

The rumors were enough to prompt Carver to remove Misty from the FBI's National Crime Information Center as a missing person. He would once again treat her as a runaway.

BOBER'S THEORY

Cory Bober's knew he was right. He knew that police would find a body of a young woman off Highway 410.

He waited but nothing happened.

Until his mother showed him the flier of Misty's disappearance.

Right again!

Heart racing, he called the number on the flier. Bober would get into contact with Diana and hurriedly told her all about his research.

He talked about the Green River Killer, where and how he killed his victims. He would tell Diana that her disappearance was connected to the same guy responsible for the murdered Puyallup Girls, Kim Delange and Anne Chebetnoy.

Cory would apologize to Diana because he knew that Misty was dead. He predicted her body would be found somewhere along Highway 410.

The two would form an uneasy alliance. Bober became Misty's personal avenger. He would start a phone/letter/media campaign to prove the police wrong and himself right.

Misty was no runaway.

She was a victim of Randall Achziger.

In October, however, Bober would be arrested for selling marijuana. He was then accosted by Sgt.Herm Carver who tired of the young man meddling in police affairs.

"He walked in the room I was being held in – looking tired and pissed off. He said, 'I got out of bed tonight, and came down here to meet you – just to see what kind of a hypocrite you REALLY ARE!'

I said (being cocky), 'It's not MY FAULT – HERM – that you don't believe Misty Copsey's MISSING!!'

He yelled (angry), 'DON'T YOU EVER CALL ME BY MY FIRST NAME – IT'S SGT. CARVER TO YOU!!!'"

Bober's journals, November 1992

THIRTY DAYS MISSING

Sgt. Herm Carver and Deputy Brian Coburn would each individually warn Diana of the troublemaker that Bober was. Still, the worried mother would welcome his assistance as she needed all the help she could get. After numerous phone calls, the two would finally meet after a month of Misty being missing. Diana had nowhere else to turn but to the shaggy-haired twenty-six-year-old who lived with his parents.

The police were going through the motions on their end. Carver reactivated Misty's name on state and national lists but only because he was legally required to do so. At this point, he still believed Misty to be a runaway and doubted Diana's veracity.

Meanwhile, Diana would find Cory Bober's constant badgering to be annoying. It got so bad she filed a restraining order against him.

"My daughter has been missing for six weeks from the Puyallup Fair," Diana wrote in the restraining order. "Cory Bober has called me on a daily basis, telling me my daughter is dead. I was advised by Deputy Brian Coburn to file this complaint if I felt threatened."

The order would only last two weeks. Diana would then call the courts and rescind her request. She would later call Bober and apologize. Her daughter had been missing for over 56 days. Bober was annoying as hell but he was the only one doing research. The only one who cared.

Bober organized a volunteer search for Misty in the Green River area. He somehow coerced someone on the police forensic team to tell him the general vicinity of where one of the Puyallup girl's body was found. Bober surmised that Misty's body would be found in the same general area.

Seventy-two days after Misty had gone missing, there was now a volunteer team searching for her.

Nothing came out of the search.

But Diana would later spot Rheuban at a grocery store and confront him. The young man ran and got into a truck with an older man. She saw the look of fear and apprehension on both men as they sped off.

Diana would then lapse into a depression. She tried to commit suicide with booze and prescription drugs.

The next day she would wake up in a hospital. She would spend the next day there, drying out until being discharged back into the nightmare that had become her life.

A PLEA TO THE PUBLIC

Four months after Misty's disappearance, Diana would appear on a local TV station for a special on the Green River Killer. Jim Doyon, the homicide detective who worked the case, spoke of the killings but deferred on stating if Delange and Chebetnoy(the slain Puyallup girls) were connected.

Doyon took an interest in Misty's case. He would journey to Highway 410 and search near milepost 30 where the bodies of Delange and Chebetnoy had been discovered.

Like Bober and the volunteer search team, he too came up empty.

Bober was undaunted and organized another search. He realized that they had been searching in the wrong spot. They were searching on the south side of the highway when the should have been searching on the north.

Twelve people would show up for the search. Diana would arrive with her older sister, Debra. Bober would arrive with Al Hensley, the father of one of the slain Puyallup girls along with his 14-year old Boy Scout nephew, Jaremy Brown.

It would be the Boy Scout that would make the find

Poking into a ditch with his stick, he saw the crumpled blue jeans. Socks fell out of the jeans.

Baggy and stone-washed, they were cuffed at the bottom. The same jeans that Misty had borrowed from her mother on the night of the fair. The jeans were too big for her and Diana remembered them cuffing them on the bottom.

Bober became excited. He knew that the killer had planted the jeans there as a taunt.

He was right. The police were wrong.

But Diana, according to her sister, "broke into a million pieces."

THE KILLING FIELD

Seven dead women had been found in the nine-mile stretch between Enumclaw and Greenwater in the eight years prior to Misty's disappearance.

The two slain Puyallup girls were found in the same area in 1988 and 1991, only one hundred feet apart. They were left off a footpath that had been hidden by thick brush.

Both of the teenage girls had been presumed abducted from the Puyallup shopping center. Detective Jim Doyon believed privately that the cases were connected. He arrived at the site where Misty's jeans were found and interviewed witnesses, particularly Diana and Bober.

The jeans were taken to the lab and the forensic analysis indicated that the jeans had been in the ditch for some time.

Police suspected that someone (Bober? Diana?) had planted the jeans there.

What was undeniable that the jeans were found only a ten minute walk away from where the bodies of the two slain Puyallup girls were found.

SUSPICIONS ARISE

People began to talk. There were reporters who believed the jeans were planted there. Some were talking as if Diana and Bober were lovers and had plotted this for some insurance money.

Dede Miles, a fifteen-year-old friend of Misty, would come to Sgt. Carver with a tip. She said there was a boy that kept coming over to Misty's parties. He would always leave before her mother came home.

His name was Rheuban Schmidt.

Finally, the unkempt looking young man would come under the radar of the police.

Diana, meanwhile, began to suspect Cory Bober.

How did he know where to look? Why was this stranger so interested in the case to begin with? How did he know so much?

The police had warned her to stay away from him. Now she felt compelled to tell the police of her suspicions.

"Diana comes to station. Now feels Cory Bober may be involved in Misty's disappearance. I asked Diana to submit a written statement to that effect and why she feels he may be involved – she agreed to do so."

Carver's notes

AN INTERVIEW WITH TRINA

Detective Jim Doyon would interview the fifteen-year-old Trina Bevard, the last person to see Misty alive.

Six months had passed. Doyon had brought along the jeans with him, the sight of which made Trina cry.

"It seems to me like something that Misty was wearing that night," Trina said. "It looks very close to what Misty was wearing. The socks, they match what she was wearing. The jeans are big, so – her jeans were baggy that night, that she was wearing. They're – they were light blue like they are in the photo. It just seems, you know, it was the clothes that she was wearing."

Doyon would go on to ask what she was wearing (a pullover) and if she had any jewelry. He then asked if she had any cigarettes or birth control pills.

"No," Trina said. "She was straight. She was a virgin. She didn't smoke, she didn't drink, she didn't do drugs. She was clean, so she had no reason to do anything. She wasn't sexually active."

Trina then revealed that the girls made five calls to Rheuban. They could not get a hold of him. They finally got him on the line and he still refused to pick them up even when the girls offered him money. Misty told him about a key under the front doormat of her home. He could go inside, get money for gas and come pick them up.

Trina stated that she didn't trust Rheuban but only because he didn't keep his word and come pick them up. She then called a 23-year old friend named Mike Rhyner for a ride but they got disconnected. The girls were then stranded. They walked downtown to get to the bus stop before spotting a phone booth by a convenience store. Misty then called her mother, telling her that if Rheuban didn't come pick her up she would take the bus. The two argued as Diana didn't want Misty around Rheuban.

Trina had to get home by 10 p.m. She had about an hour and a half to get home which wasn't that far. Misty could not walk the ten miles to Spanaway.

Trina then decided to walk. She gave Misty her extra money for the bus.

"At that time I made my decision of walking home and she said she would take the bus," Trina recalled. "The last words that I said to her were 'Be careful,' and she turned around and told me the same and we walked off in different directions"

Trina also dismissed the notion of Misty being a runaway.

" Her mom just bought her a stereo and she was so excited and she went shopping and she got new clothes,"Trina recalled. She was telling me all about it. She was really excited about it.

BOBER GOES TO JAIL

Meanwhile, Bober would be sentenced to fourteen months in prison for the marijuana possession. He felt that the sentencing was too punitive and threatened law enforcement that they would never find Misty without him. His fellow inmates thought he was crazy and began calling him "snitch" and "The Green River Killer".

Jail would not slow down Bober's efforts, however. He continued to research and write Misty's mother.

"Dear Diana,

...When we found Misty's clothes, part of me died and I watched a part of you die too (much more than a "part") and I was at a total loss for words. I never wanted to be the one to show you your most horrible fears were true and that your daughter is truly dead at the hands of a sick murderer. I will never rest until the killer (Randy Achziger) is brought to justice and dead, if it takes my life to do it."

AMERICA'S MOST WANTED

Misty's case would eventually be broadcast nationally as it was featured on the America's Most Wanted television show.

Over twenty-eight tips came into Sgt. Carver from people who watched the broadcast.

When the tips went nowhere, Diana's suspicions returned to her original suspect, Rheuban Schmidt. She wanted Carver to speak to the young man but the Sergeant would take a circuitous route to get to Schmidt.

Carver would speak to Frank Rodriguez, the owner of Adam's Ribs, a restaurant where Rheuban worked. He convinced the owner to try and find out how much Rheuban knew about Misty.

"3-4-93 @ 1500: Frank states Rheuban said the following during a lengthy conversation about Misty Copsey:

- Yeah, I know about it.
- I know exactly where she is buried.
- They found the clothes but she is buried 6 miles from there.
- They're off by 6 or 6 1/2 miles."

— Excerpt from Carver's notes

Carver would then wait for Rheuban outside the restaurant before his shift started. Schmidt arrived, saw the cops and immediately ran off. The detectives would eventually catch up with him.

Rheuban would concede that he had received calls from Misty the night of her disappearance. But his story corroborated with Trina's, he told the girls he had no gas and could not pick them up.

Carver then asked if he knew where Misty was buried but Rheuban was adamant that he "said those things to get Frank off my back."

Rheuban then revealed that he suffered from "black outs". He stated that he did not recall anything until the daylight hours of September 18th, 1992.

The detectives pounced, asking if it was possible that he blacked out, picked up Misty and harmed her.

Rheuban claimed he didn't know.

All he knew was that he drove out to his grandmother's farmhouse and couldn't recall why.

Detectives would then give Rheuban a polygraph test.

They would later state that the suspect "zoned out" during the test, nearly falling asleep. The tests were inconclusive but detectives felt as if he were trying to beat the test.

A LITTLE LIE

Rheuban fell off the detective's radar when Carver talked to Dede Miles again. Dede would tell the detective that Trina had not walked home from the fairground like she told him.

Dede said that Trina had a boyfriend come pick her up and didn't want anyone to know.

Trina's boyfriend's name was Michael J. Rhyner. He had nothing on his record aside from traffic stops but he had friends that were connected with Chebetnoy and Delange.

He also had a complaint when he was sixteen years old. He was accused of an abduction rape wherein he used a knife and a cigarette lighter to terrorize an eleven-year-old.

Charges were never filed for an undisclosed reason.

Carver brought Trina in for more questioning. He wanted the truth. The truth about who picked her up that night. The truth about Misty.

But the truth was that Trina told the Sgt. Carver and Detective Tom Matison that she lied because she feared "getting into trouble with her guardian about it."

Trina admitted that she called Rhyner, got disconnected and left a message. She told Misty that they could both ride with Rhyner but Misty said no.

"Trina would not be specific why Misty did not trust Rhyner, but the indication was that Rhyner might have 'come on' to Misty at one time and she did not like it. Trina states that she and Rhyner are friends, but not involved."

— Matison's notes

Trina said that she started to walk and then Rhyner picked her up and dropped her off. The detectives asked if perhaps Rhyner had picked up Misty but she said no.

FRANK RODRIGUEZ' FOLLOW UP

Diana would state that Frank Rodriguez, Rheuban's employer, would call her to say that Rheuban had "bragged about doing something" to Misty with his uncle. Frank didn't fully believe him, however, as Rheuban was "weird" and always bragging about stuff he didn't do.

Diana then approached Carver about Rheuban and the sergeant went ballistic.

"We have our man!" he said.

The man he sought was Michael Rhyner, Trina Bevard's boyfriend.

"We share our knowledge of Mike Rhyner and how he is involved with Misty and Trina – and the fact Trina lied to Doyon. We state that there is an excellent possibility that Rhyner may be linked to Chebetnoy and DeLange. Exchange of information is extremely beneficial."

— Carver's notes

"Sgt. Carver believes that Rhyner dropped Bevard off, returned to the area of the fairgrounds, located Misty Copsey, convinced her to get into his vehicle and drove off with her."

— Doyon's notes

Police set up a sting on Rhyner. The car mechanic was selling his 1981 blue Ford Escort for $200 bucks.

The buyer was an undercover cop.

He watched as Rhyner hurriedly took out trash from the car before the sale. The police then did a forensic examination of the car.

Meanwhile, Rheuban's green Nova was being crushed at a wrecking yard. The Puyallup police didn't care as the tweaker was no longer on their radar. Also, Randy Achziger, Bober's suspect, had been charged and convicted for the rape of a seven-year-old.

INTERROGATING RHYNER

Ideally, Detectives Matison and Sgt. Carver wanted the forensics back from Rhyner's Escort before they spoke to him. But the wait became interminable and they brought him in for questioning without some evidence to back up their suspicions.

Rhyner's story would match that of Trina's. He picked Trina up and went back home. He said that he and Trina were only "good friends" and he had met Misty only four times. Matison then asked Rhyner if he felt Misty was alive and what should happen to the person who harmed her.

Rhyner knew what the detective was getting at. On his own volition, Rhyner told the detectives about his juvenile complaint from years ago. He stated he had been cleared and knew that was why they were looking at him now.

"First thing I thought, you know, well, that's in my file," Rhyner said. "Now you guys are going to think I did it since it's in my file. About Misty, that's the one thing that worried me."

Rhyner then passed a polygraph test.

Grasping at straws, the police then turned their sights back on Rheuban. If only they had impounded his car when they had the chance...

TOO LITTLE TOO LATE

"Rheuban Schmidt's initial interview with Sgt. Carver and I created more questions than answers. He was very vague about what he did that September 17th and finally said that he had a 'blackout' and 'woke up' at his grandmother's property near Enumclaw.

...Schmidt had told Frank Rodriguez that Misty's body was six miles from where the jeans were found. He now claims that he said this just to get Rodriguez "off his back," and was not a true statement.

He was driving a Green Chev Nova at the time but he no longer has the vehicle. It was repossessed.

Schmidt also mentioned that his Grandmother's property is located in King County by Buckley and is over a hundred acres. The property has cows on it. Few people enter onto the property."

— Matison's notes

Tinsley, fifteen years old at the time of Misty's disappearance, told police the Rheuban was his roommate for only a few months. He described Rheuban as a short-tempered guy who had a thirteen-year-old girlfriend. The girlfriend, Tinsley said, got jealous when Rheuban got a call from Misty.

Tinsley stated that Rheuban had left the apartment in a huff then came back between eleven and one at night.

So Rheuban did not "black out" as he told detectives. N

"What do you think might have happened to her?" Matison asked.

"Um, I couldn't, I couldn't say because I have no idea," Tinsley said.

"Well, can you speculate?"

"With Rheuban, this is just that I, this, this is what I say with Rheuban because I, I figure that um that he, he tried to, he tried to um, get with her or something and she said, she said no and he got all pissed and did something, I don't know, that's just a second guess."

"You think Rheuban would be capable of ah, kidnapping and killing somebody?"

"I think he could," Tinsley said.

Detectives would meet with Rheuban again, relaying the information that Tinsley recalled him coming back to the apartment that night.

But Rheuban remained adamant in stating that he didn't remember what he did. The detectives then drove him out to his grandmother's farm which had over 100-acres...100 secluded acres.

Detective Matison would note that Rheuban's grandmother's house six miles north of Buckley. Rheuban told Frank that Misty would be buried six miles away from where her jeans were found which would place it in the close vicinity of his grandmother's farm. They would go to inquire with his grandmother but she was not home.

They did not follow-up with the grandmother .

Even so, Rheuban's story no longer held up. He told Misty that he didn't have any gas. He lived sixteen miles away from the fair.

But then he stated that he had driven to his grandmother's farm in Buckley then returned home.

A sixty-mile round trip.

Detectives would give him another polygraph test which he passed.

"It appears that Rheuban Schmidt was not involved in the disappearance of Misty Copsey. He, however, has no alibi as to his movements during the evening of her disappearance, as well as no memory; he claimed that he had a blackout. He acknowledges that he left the residence of James Tinsley, but does not remember what he did.

Investigation to continue."

— Matison's notes

ONE YEAR ANNIVERSARY

The local media ran a few more stories on Misty's disappearance as the Puyallup Fair started. The forensic test on Rhyner's test finally came through. There was no match

with Misty anywhere.

Now once again grasping at straws, Carver would turn to Diana and her associates. He would interview Diana's parole officer and one of her ex-boyfriends.

Misty's father, Buck, was asked to take a polygraph test. He gave consent and passed.

"I explained to her that missing person investigations, at some point in time, must eliminate the parents of any wrongdoing. Diana agreed to the examination."

— Carver's notes

Diana would pass her polygraph test but Jim Corey, Doyon's colleague, said that Diana's polygraph would prove to be inconclusive and that perhaps she had something to do with planting the jeans at the location on Hwy 410.

Carver had always had his doubts about Diana and felt that she planted the jeans.

But the leads would eventually dry up. After nine years, Misty Copsey's disappearance would turn cold.

No one was ever charged with her disappearance.

THE AFTERMATH

Diana would hand out fliers at the Puyallup Fairgrounds every year. She was doing more than law enforcement and even the media.

Every now and then, a local reporter would run a story about Misty. A few cranks would call in and say that they knew something but it would lead to nowhere. Then that would be it. Everything would run dry.

Detective Jim Doyon felt that she was deceased.

BOBER TO THE RESCUE

Bober was then caught for marijuana possession again but this time, he pressed for an advantage. He would gain the Washington State Patrol crime lab report on Misty's jeans, compiled after their 1993 discovery.

He argued that the lab report was part of his defense....he gambled and won.

Obtaining the prized document, the amateur sleuth went to work. The report stated there was no blood, no semen. But there were hairs, fibers, and three red paint chips. There were also holes in the left leg in the jeans, above the knee.

Bober knew that somehow, someway, Randy Achziger was involved. That he killed Misty.

The forensic details raced through Bober's head...red paint chips...red paint chips...

He knew that Bober had a red Porsche. He knew that the paint chips would match.

But the police had another suspect they didn't tell anyone about.

Robert Leslie Hickey.

Hickey's hunting ground was the Puyallup area where he specialized in abduction rapes.

He also drove a red Camaro.

Puyallup police had him on their list as a possible suspect but he was never questioned nor did they obtain forensic samples from his car.

Thirteen years later, however, they would collect samples from Achziger's old car. The car had been sold and the new owner was open to having forensics performed on it.

The particles would be sent to a crime lab which already had a backlog of over a year.

With nothing else left to do, the police turned once again to Rheuban Schmidt.

"I think it's worth taking another shot at Schmidt, and we're planning on it. He's been clean since 1993 ...

— Excerpt from notes by Lt. Dave McDonald, March 19, 2006

Only Schmidt had not been clean. He had been convicted of second-degree theft in 2000. In early 1996, he was accused of rape by one of Misty's best friends. He had held a pillow over her face to silence her but two weeks after filing the report, the girl back away from her accusation and did not file charges.

"[She] told me that she would be undergoing counseling related to the rape, but that she did not want to undergo any additional stress that may be caused by further investigation or possible prosecution in this matter.

Case cleared exceptional/refused by victim."

— Pierce County sheriff's report, Feb. 6, 1996

Later in 2006, Puyallup police gathered more reports on Rheuban. One was a domestic violence protection order requested by his wife, the mother of his three children.

"Rheuban has previously told her that if she ever had him served with a court order he'd 1) burn her house down with her and her kids in it, and 2) send 'some guys' to kick in her door and take money from her.

(She) said Rheuban told her that they'd get money from her if they had to beat her, rape her and then rob her.

(She) said Rheuban told her that if it came to that she 'wouldn't be breathing' when they were done with her."

— Pierce County Sheriff's report, Nov. 9, 2006

MISSING PAINT CHIPS

Adding more incompetence to the investigation, the red paint chips found on Misty's jeans would turn up "missing." All that remained inside the bag where the chips were marked was a piece of plastic.

The lab technicians now had no way to match the red chips on Misty's jeans to Achziger's red Porsche.

Bober would claim that the red chips did match and the police were now trying to save face. Diana, however, no longer wants anything to do with him.

Bober would state that the police would tell Diana that they had, in fact, tested the red paint found on Misty's clothes against Achziger's Porsche. Bober discovered that the red paint was missing beforehand yet the police would lie to Diana about the test.

The lies and incompetence that began investigation have seemingly ended it as well. The Puyallup police relied far too heavily on polygraph tests to discount suspects where their own accounts (particularly in the case of Schmidt) were shaky at best. They failed to secure possession of Schmidt's Green Nova which may have proven to provide forensic evidence that Misty was in his vehicle.

Twenty-four years have elapsed since Misty's disappearance.

Her case remains unsolved.

THE CHOWCHILLA KIDNAPPINGS

105

KAREN HULSE

Chowchilla is a large farming community located about forty miles north of Fresno, California, in the dead center of the state. Named after the war-mongering nature of the area's American Indian settlers, the Yokuts, the name 'Chowchilla' translates to "murderers". Tributes to the Yokuts are still very present throughout Chowchilla, in art, school mascots, and tourist attractions.

Dwarfed next to other cities in the San Francisco Bay Area, Chowchilla drew little interest from anyone who was not a local or simply passing through to get to the coast. Chowchilla has no beautiful coastline to attract visitors or any notable industries like Silicon Valley. But it has instead maintained a small town feel through much of the 20th century as the surrounding area was booming with tech industry growth and skyrocketing housing prices.

Chowchilla's population has grown to over 18,000 and is home to several prisons and school districts. However, just forty years ago the town was home to less than 5,000 people. The small town community in 1970's Chowchilla made the events of July 15th, 1976, even more surprising than it otherwise would have been. After all, no one expected twenty-six grade schoolchildren to be kidnapped and buried alive in such a quiet farming neighborhood.

The Bus Ride Home

On the afternoon of July 15th, 1976, the Chowchilla summer school program was about to wrap up. During the summer months, the children were kept busy and out of the house with arts and crafts, swimming, and games in the park. Twenty-six children from the small farming town, ranging in age from 5 to 14 years old, came and went from the Dairyland Elementary School by school bus.

July 15th was to be the second-to-last scheduled day of the program for the summer, but the children had been having so much fun during the past few weeks that they crafted a petition to extend the program through the end of the month. The program was so popular that even the summer school teachers and the children's bus driver, Frank Edward "Ed" Ray, agreed to sign the petition for the children.

That morning was bright and sunny, so the children and their teachers had spent the day in the local community pool. Everyone swam and played with water balloons. On the bus ride home, many of the children were still wearing their damp bathing suits while others were wrapped up in beach towels. The bus ride home was filled with excitement over the potential for another couple weeks of summer school.

Everyone was happy and the adults had their guard down. School bus driver Ed was not overly suspicious when their path was blocked by a crippled van in the middle of the lane. They were driving down a narrow gravel road and he slowed as he came upon the van with its hood propped up. Since he was unable to easily pass the van, and due to the neighborly community that was Chowchilla at the time, Ed stopped the bus in order to offer help to the stranded travelers. Unfortunately for him and the children, this friendly gesture would be the beginning of a daylong nightmare for them all.

Kidnapped in Broad Daylight

As he brought the school bus to a stop, Ed opened the passenger doors to offer assistance to the drivers of the disabled van. But before he could even finish his offer, three men ambushed the bus with a rifle, handguns, and pantyhose pulled over their faces to obscure their appearance.

These three men were Fred Woods, Rick Schoenfeld, and Jim Schoenfeld. Rick and Jim were brothers and close friends with Fred, three desperate men looking to get rich without any consequence. Somewhere along their planning process, one of the men had crafted the harebrained scheme of kidnapping the community's young children and holding them hostage for ransom. Now here they were, ambushing a school bus full of young, terrified children who had just moments earlier been basking in the glow of a sunshiny day with their friends.

Fred, Rick, and Jim forced Ed into the back of the bus, as far away from the kidnappers as possible. With the one real threat to their plan trapped in the back of the bus, the three armed men took control of the wheel and began to drive the bus filled with children and the bus driver to an unknown location.

The children were terrified. Lynda Carrejo Labendeira, seated toward the front of the bus and just inches away from the men and their loaded guns, hid under her seat as the bus bumped across back roads and through bamboo thickets. Her three sisters were crying and panicked in the back of the bus while the rest of the schoolchildren sobbed, fearing for their lives.

They continued to drive through thick bamboo, tossing the bus from side-to-side with each stalk that the bus hit. The children continued to cower in fear as the school bus bumped and swayed through the thickets until eventually they arrived at a hidden ditch. Here, Ed and the children saw two vans parked in the small clearing, waiting for their arrival.

A Road Trip of Nightmares

The school bus stopped and the three men once again pointed their weapons at the children. Everyone, including Ed, were instructed to get into the back of the vans.

The windows of the vans were all painted black. The children could not see where they were and no one from the outside could see the abductees kept captive inside the vehicles.

It was a hot day, over one hundred degrees outside and the children had to relieve themselves.

Hours passed as the children grew hungry, sick, and the heat only amplified all of the sour smells filling the back of the vans. The children were dehydrated and ill, and no one knew what was going to happen when the vans eventually did stop.

For countless hours and miles, the vans continued to drive. Ed believed that the men were either taking them to a predetermined location or they were trying to stall for time. After what felt like an interminable drive, the vans finally came to a stop.

The kidnappers had arrived at their destination, a rock quarry in Livermore, California near San Francisco.

Buried Alive

The California Rock & Gravel Quarry was owner and operated by Fred Woods' father. The business was a busy one, but at night the grounds were entirely empty.

Under the dim illumination of construction lights, Fred, Rick, and Jim ordered everyone out of the now foul-smelling vans. The children and Ed pleaded with the men to explain what they were doing or where they were, but the only response they ever received was a rough, "Shut up and be quiet."

The children and Ed stumbled out of their cramped prisons into the quarry, and one-by-one their captors ordered each child to provide their name, age, address, and home phone number. After this information had been written down, the child was stripped of a single piece of clothing, to serve as proof of their hostages.

The armed men led their hostages through the empty quarry to a moving van buried under the quarry's surface. The van was hidden underground and nearly invisible from the surface, and the only way in or out of the cavity was by a long ladder.

It looked like one big coffin.

Once again pointing their weapons at the children, the three men ordered everyone down the ladder into the buried moving van. Each child carefully descended the ladder into the dusty, dark van, and once the last one had finished the journey, the men removed the ladder, blocked the door, and left.

An Underground Prison Cell

The buried moving van was stocked with only a few crude items, and not nearly enough to provide the hostages with any amount of comfort. There was old cereal, peanut butter, bread, and bottled water, but only enough of each to feed the children one pathetic meal. After going all day without food or water, these items did little to comfort the sickness overtaking most of the children.

There were several dirty mattresses scattered across the cell's floor, which frightened the children as they took them as a sign that they would be held in this underground prison for days or longer. A makeshift toilet was available in the form of a crude hole cut into the bottom of the moving van, but this offered little relief to the children.

The armed men had installed ventilation fans in the van's walls, in an attempt to keep the captives alive underground. However, several hours into the children's' captivity these fans failed and the prison cell began to fill with odors and fumes.

Many of the children were finally overcome by their sickness, and the smell of vomit, urine, and feces filled the airtight compartment. As hours passed, the children began to cry and scream, wishing for their parents to find them. With the little available food completely gone and conditions worsening, the hostages slowly began to accept that they might not ever leave this prison cell beneath the quarry.

The Last Hope

As the younger children succumbed to their exhaustion, sickness, and panic, Ed and the older children began to craft a last ditch plan to escape the underground holding cell. On the ceiling of the moving van was a removable metal panel, which offered the only chance the children and their bus driver had of escaping their prison. They began to drag the dirty mattresses across the van, piling them up underneath the panel. One by one, they drew closer to reaching the potential escape route.

Unfortunately, once they could reach the panel, they found that it was barricaded on top with a heavy truck battery and several feet of piled dirt. Together, Ed and the oldest of the boys pushed with all their strength, hoping to break free of the weight above them.

Finally, the panel shifted, and Ed and the boys were able to reach the dirt above them. The boys helped dig out the dirt piled above them, as the younger children watched or hid in case the captors returned. Many were afraid that they would be standing outside, watching for any attempt to escape from the underground prison. Despite the opportunity for escape, a palpable fear was in the air. If the men returned, the children were smart enough to realize they would be shot.

Exhausted and covered in dirt and filth, Ed and the boys finally broke free to the surface. They began lifting the younger children out of the moving van, with some standing on each other's shoulder in order to reach the escape panel. One by one, they emerged on the surface, and the hostages suddenly found themselves free after hours of torture, illness, and panic.

The group cautiously maneuvered the quarry, unsure of where their captors were hiding. Fortunately for Ed and the children, the three armed men were asleep during the entire escape. Thanks to a poorly timed nap, the kidnappers lost their hostages without any idea what was happening.

As they frantically searched for help, the group of children noticed a small building overlooking the quarry. One of the children, Lynda Carrejo Labendeira, recalled that they found a man at one of the buildings.

"The gentleman came down and said, 'The world's been looking for you.'" With the entire community of Chowchilla searching for their missing children, news had spread far and wide in hopes of finding the children and their bus driver safe and sound.

With the help of this man, the authorities were alerted and medical help was sent to the quarry. The children were cleaned up and any dehydration or illness was treated. By July 17th, everyone had been returned home safely, where the families of the children welcomed them home with open arms.

The Hunt for the Kidnappers

At first, authorities had few leads to who might have kidnapped the children and their bus driver on July 15th. While Woods and the Schoenfeld brothers had attempted several times to call the local police with their ransom note, asking for $5 million for the safe return of the town's beloved children, so many frantic calls had been coming into the local dispatch station that they couldn't even get through to speak to authorities. Because they were never actually able to deliver their demands to the police, law enforcement were unsure of the motive when beginning their investigation.

With few leads, the police turned to an unusual tactic. Ed, the bus driver who had been held captive with the children, was put under hypnosis in an attempt to remember the license plate of one of the vans used to transport the group to the quarry and their underground prison. Miraculously, Ed did remember one of the plate numbers, which was traced back to the quarry owner's son, Fred Woods.

Fred Woods was arrested after running away from authorities and attempting to hide out in Vancouver, Canada. His partners, Rick and Jim Schoenfeld, surrendered to authorities while still in California, after hearing that their accomplice had been arrested.

When investigating the trio, the police found a drafted ransom note, presumably what the men would have read to police if they had ever gotten through on the phone lines. They also found evidence that the men might have been inspired by High Pentecost's The Day the Children Vanished, which might have recently been checked out from the Chowchilla Public Library by one of the men.

All three men were from wealthy, privileged San Francisco Bay area families, and had no real reason to commit such a crime for money. Connections to child pornography, acts of violence, and other signs point to the fact that the three men were a twisted group of friends without a firm grip on their consciences. Jim Schoenfeld told commissioners that the ransom was dreamed up because he was in debt and jealous of the "Ferraris" and other luxuries that his neighbors owned. Woods stated that he didn't need the money, because he owned and operated a fruitful auto yard, but that his involvement in the crime was just motivated by greed. Either way, the men planned their kidnapping and ransom of the children for over a year before actually committing the crime.

Punishment for the Kidnappers

After their trial, each of the three kidnappers pleaded guilty to twenty-seven life sentences without the option of parole. Yet now, in 2017, only one of these men remains behind bars. Rick was released in 2012, and his brother Jim was given parole in 2015. Fred Woods currently remains in prison and is ineligible for parole until 2018. Ever since the first Schoenfeld brother was released from prison, tension has risen among the Chowchilla community. But there are none as concerned as the now-adult victims of these men.

"We felt safe in Chowchilla," said Lynda Carrejo Labendeira, now a grown woman with a family of her own. She was referring to the fact that, for many years, everyone in Chowchilla felt safe knowing that the terrible men that had kidnapped twenty-six of their community's young children would be stuck behind bars forever. The kidnappers' lifetime imprisonment was a comfort to their victims, who were terrified of what the men might be capable of if released from their sentences.

Unfortunately, all three of the men were granted eligibility for parole when an appeals court reviewed their sentences. The reasoning for this decision was that Woods and the Schoenfeld brothers did no physical bodily harm to the children or bus driver that they held hostage for over eighteen hours.

The Schoenfeld brothers have both been freed from prison at this time. Many of the victims and their families feel that the victims' emotional wellbeing has been completely overlooked in the decision to release these criminals.

Woods' Parole Trial

The Schoenfeld brothers' attorney advocates for the eventual release of Woods, claiming that he is no danger to his past victims. However, with a past of rule breaking, child pornography, and illicit cell phone use, Woods' chances of being paroled in the near future are slim-to-none. With the other two kidnappers out free on the streets, this is little comfort to the community of Chowchilla.

In 2015, Woods was eligible to apply for parole. Unlike his accomplices, though, this venture was not successful. Citing Woods' many "disciplinary infractions" while in prison, as well as three instances of possession of pornography, some of it featuring minors, and two instances of possessing a contraband phone, Jill Klinge, an attorney in Alameda County, did not believe that Woods deserved parole.

David Linn, the District Attorney for Madera County, where Chowchilla is located, mentioned that because of Woods' "privileged background" the convict was unwilling to follow the rules – of life or of prison. Linn also credited some of the kidnapping victims who had come forward at the trial for Wood's denial of parole, stating that they had given statements that "tugged at the heartstrings."

Despite the overwhelming disdain for Woods, his parole drew many noteworthy supporters. Palo Alto Representative Anna Eshoo wrote to the court stating that Woods had "paid his debt to society." Even some of the kidnapping victims said that they believed Woods had served his time and deserved to rejoin society.

Lasting Effects

Life after the kidnapping has been very rough for many of the children. Symptoms of P.T.S.D. are rampant throughout the twenty-six children. Many of them report experiencing panic attacks and nightmares for years after the kidnapping actually occurred. One even shot a tourist with BB gun when the man parked his car outside of the survivor's home. Decades after the kidnapping, several of the children suffer from substance abuse problems or have spent time in prison for behavioral issues, much of which has been linked to the trauma experienced in their childhood.

After committing the largest kidnapping in United States history, there was little mercy available to Woods and the Schoenfeld brothers. After decades in prison, they are now being presented with a lawsuit pursued by many of their victims from the kidnapping in 1976. This lawsuit is meant to reflect the immense emotional trauma that the children underwent during their kidnapping at gunpoint and subsequent imprisonment.

Jennifer Hyde, who is now almost fifty years old, told the media that she is still afraid of the dark decades after the kidnapping occurred. In fact, until very recently, she could only sleep when there was a nightlight on in her bedroom. She also reported having nightmares where she died and was attending or one funeral, which she connected to the belief that she was going to die that day in the buried moving truck.

Hyde also claims that her family suffers from her experience as a child. "[My] children don't get to lead a normal life," she said, which she blames on the fact she is overprotective and terrified of something similar happening to her own children as what happened to her in 1976. When her first child started kindergarten, Hyde skipped work everyday to follow her son's school bus and ensure that he arrived safely at a friend's house.

Remembering a Hero

Edward "Ed" Ray, the children's bus driver and the man largely responsible for their escape, was awarded a citation for outstanding community service, and February 26th is officially Edward Ray Day in Chowchilla, California. Many of the children he helped rescue that day continued to keep in touch and visit him until his death on May 17th, 2012.

Without the help of Ed that day, who knows what would have happened to the children. While the events of July 15th, 1976, might be near-forgotten in the minds of many Chowchilla residents, it would be a travesty to let the heroic actions of Ed Ray become nothing more than a story told in the history books. When faced with a dangerous threat, whether it is a man with a gun or a wild animal, it truly says something about a man whether he protects himself first or acts in order to protect those who depend on him. On July 15ht, 1976, Edward "Ed" Ray was the latter.

The Chowchilla Kidnappings in Pop Culture

While the kidnapping may have been inspired by a short story itself, many replications of the events have appeared in television and movies. An episode of Walker, Texas Ranger, starring Chuck Norris, involved a school bus kidnapping that closely matched the real-life events in Chowchilla. A made-for-television, full-length film called They've Taken Our Children was a popular telling of the Chowchilla kidnappings. The events of July 15th, 1976, have also been covered on countless true crime television programs throughout the years.

The Chinchilla kidnapping, while certainly not the most famous true crime in history, has become one of many tropes when it comes to almost-too-ridiculous-to-be-true scenarios found on primetime television shows. While the Chinchilla kidnappings may not be referenced directly, situations where crowds of people, whether students on a school bus or commuters on a train are kidnapped as a group are commonly seen on shows like CSI, Without a Trace, and NCIS.

Chowchilla Today

Now, many of Chowchilla's citizens think little of the kidnapping that occurred over 40 years ago. Because of Chowchilla's quick growth, the majority of its current residents either moved to Chowchilla after 1976, or were not born or old enough to remember the hysteria that erupted around the traumatic incident. Most people who were alive during the kidnapping only think of that day when news reports mention anniversaries or trials for the kidnappers. But for the victims, who are now almost all adults with children of their own, the events of their childhood come to mind every single day.

Many of the children who were kidnapped that day, including Jennifer Hyde, have moved out of Chowchilla or California. Some are running away from the memories of their childhood, while others have moved for less sinister reasons like career opportunities or family. Sadly for Hyde, her brother, Jeff Hyde, who was also kidnapped from the school bus that day, was killed in an accident at the age of fifteen. With a childhood filled with tragic events, it is no wonder that Jennifer Hyde left her hometown.

It is understandable why the city of Chowchilla doesn't want to dwell on the events of over forty years ago, and instead wants to move on and paint a new image of itself for the nation. The kidnapping has now become part of history. Everyone made it back home to his or her family, and that is that. However, this doesn't erase the events of July 15th, 1976, from the past, and, while the only sources that bring up the kidnapping at this point are true crime enthusiasts and media reporters, the kidnapping of twenty-six schoolchildren from a bus remains a vivid part of the town's history.

THE MISSING BEAUMONT CHILDREN

It was a warm summer morning on January 26, 1966, when the three Beaumont children left their suburban home to celebrate Australia Day at the beach. The children regularly made the trip by themselves, so their mother felt at ease providing them with bus fare and sending them on their way while she visited and had lunch with a close friend. However, she would return home that afternoon to find that the children still had not returned. That morning would end up being the last time she saw her three children.

Jane (aged 9), Arnna (aged 7), and Grant (aged 4), lived in Somerton Park, a quiet suburb minutes away from Adelaide, South Australia. Their father, Jim Beaumont, was a linen goods salesman who frequently traveled for work and their mother, Nancy Beaumont, was a stay-at-home mother.

The oldest child, Jane, was viewed by her parents as responsible enough to supervise the other children for short trips and adventures, a style of parenting that was the norm in Australia at that time. The children frequently took the five-minute bus ride to neighboring Glenely Beach by themselves and were looking forward to celebrating the national holiday at the beach.

The children left their home at 10:00am that morning and were seen arriving at the beach by witnesses at 10:15am. They spent much of that morning at play on the beach and were supposed to arrive home at 2:00pm. When they did not arrive at the appointed time, their mother assumed that they had become preoccupied with celebrating the holiday with their playmates and that they would arrive on the next bus or had decided to walk home, something that the three children had done before. When the children did not disembark from the next scheduled bus, their mother began to grow worried.

The disappearance of the Beaumont children would result in one of the largest manhunts and police investigations in Australian history. Furthermore, the event had widespread consequences on Australian society, shattering the illusion that many parents had regarding their children's safety and changing the way that Australians parented their children forever.

Timeline of Events

10:00am - The children leave their Somerton Park home to travel to Glenely Beach by bus.

10:15am - They are seen exiting the bus by multiple witnesses.

11:00am - The three children are spotted playing beneath a sprinkler by an elderly woman. A tall blond man is spotted lying on the ground next to them, watching the children play.

11:15am - A tall blond man is seen playing with the children. They all appear to be laughing and at ease.

11:45am - The children purchase several pastries and a meat pie from the beach snack shop.

12:15pm - The tall blond man and the children are seen leaving the beach together. The children are witnessed laughing together and holding hands.

3:00pm - A postman on his route spots the children walking along Jetty Road alone, away from the beach. The postman is known to the children and they exchange greetings. Police believe that the timeline for this event is incorrect.

7:20pm - The parents of the children become gravely concerned and file a missing children's report with the local police department. Jim Beaumont and the local police search the entire Glenely Beach area.

8:40pm - Police search the surrounding beaches with no results. The father contacts friends and relatives in an attempt to locate the children.

10:00pm - Police issue public radio announcements with a missing children report.

Points of Interest

There are several details in this story which raised doubts with both the parents of the children and the local police department. When the children departed for Glenely Beach in the morning of January 26th, they left with only enough money to cover their bus fare: six shilling and a sixpence. However, the shop owner, who sold several pastries and a meat pie to the children at 11:45am, reported that the children paid for the food with a $1 bill, an amount of money that they did not have when they left their mother's care.

In addition, the shop owner knew the children well and had sold them food and pastries several times before. He reported that the children had never purchased a meat pie before. This suggests that the children received the money from someone after leaving their parents home and that they may have been purchasing the meat pie for someone else.

Lastly, the mother of the children, Nancy Beaumont, repeatedly said that her children were quite shy and very unlikely to speak with strangers, indicating that they may have met the tall blond man prior to the date of their disappearance. Their mother also remembered a seemingly innocuous comment from Arnna, who had previously told her mother that Jane had "got a boyfriend down the beach." Nancy assumed that her daughter was referring to a young playmate, but in hindsight it seems that she may have been referring to the tall blond man spotted by witnesses.

Police Investigation

The South Australian police force began investigating the disappearance of the children in full-force the evening of their disappearance. After interviewing several witnesses who were present at Glenely Beach, they were able to determine that the children were playing with a tall blond, "thin-faced" man while at the beach. He was described as being a blond man in his late 30s with a thin or athletic build.

"Things seemed bungled from the get-go," forensic psychologist Paula Orange said. "First off, the artist drawing the picture admitted to being drunk at the time of completing his task. So the sketch made of the suspect looks more like a lantern-jawed alien than a real person. Secondly, the witnesses claimed that the man was in his late thirties. Witnesses are notorious for getting ages wrong and the police dismissed too many possible subjects out of hand because they didn't fit the profile."

Several witnesses stated that the man was seen dressing the children prior to leaving the beach. The children's parents said that the kids, especially Jane, were very shy and unlikely to speak to a stranger. This later led police to theorize that the children had met the man in question prior to the date of their disappearance and had grown to know him over a period of several weeks.

The blond man and three children were seen leaving the beach together at 12:15pm, after the children purchased several pastries and a meat pie from a local vendor with a $1 bill, an amount of money that they did not have when they left their home that morning.

A wrench was thrown into the investigation when a postman, who knew the children and was on friendly terms with them, reported that he saw the children around 3:00pm that afternoon walking away from the beach and in the direction of their home in Somerton Park. He stated that he exchanged greetings with the young children and that they seemed to be in good spirits. In particular, the postman said that he say the children were "holding hands and laughing" as they walked down the road alone, with no blond companion in sight. Police later said that they believed the postman was mistaken about the timeline and that he most likely saw the children walking some time before noon.

Several months later, a woman in a nearby neighborhood contacted police and told them that she had seen a man with two girls and a young boy enter an abandoned house on her street. She also reported seeing the young boy walking away from the house before he was roughly grabbed by, and returned to the house with, the older man. She never saw the man or children again.

"The response from the public was overwhelming," Orange said. "People drove from miles away to aid in the search. They combed the beach and drained part of it all to no avail. They found nothing, not a trace."

The police were quickly able to eliminate drowning as the cause of the children's disappearance as a result of several witnesses saying that they saw the children leave the beach around 12:15pm. Furthermore, all of the children's belongings were missing, lending further support to the theory that they left the beach. After speaking with the parents, the police were able to identify seventeen different items that were carried by the children that day, providing a list of items that could be used to identify their remains or whereabouts. However, the police's continue efforts continued to prove fruitless.

The Psychic Circus

On November 8, 1966, nearly a year after the children's initial disappearance, an internationally-renowned psychic from the Netherlands, Gerard Croiset, was flown to Australia to investigate the case. His presence caused a whirlwind of media coverage in Australia and across the world. After making a series of outlandish and ever-changing claims, Croiset claimed that the children were buried underneath a warehouse just minutes away from the children's school.

"I appreciate him (Gerard Croiset) coming out to find the children," Jim Beaumont said. "But I don't believe what he said. I don't believe the children are dead and will continue to believe until given evidence that proves otherwise."

The building, which was under construction at the time of their disappearance, was eventually razed and excavated after the owners raised $40,000 for the project as a result of public pressure. No evidence of the children or their belongings were ever found.

"The press and police followed Croiset around everywhere," Orange said. "He was an obvious con artist but they were desperate. They had nothing."

A Series of Letters

Beginning in 1968, the parents of the three children began to receive a series of letters which rekindled hope in the idea that their children may still be alive. Postmarked from Dandernong, Victoria, the series of letters claimed to be written by Jane, the eldest daughter. She claimed to be under the supervision of a man and in good health and care, saying

Dear Mum and Dad,

We had a beautiful lunch today...The man is feeding us really well. The man took us to see The Sound of Music yesterday.

Police officers believed the letters to be from Jane after comparing them to examples of her handwriting and, as far as 1981, the Sidney Morning Herald produced analysis from handwriting experts claiming that the letters were actually from the missing child.

Following receipt of the letters supposedly sent from Jane, the parents received a letter from a man claiming to be in possession of the children. He said that he was willing to hand the children over to the parents at a specific time and location. The Beaumonts arrived at the appointed time and location with an undercover police officer but no one showed. They later received a letter from the same man claiming that he saw the undercover police officer arrive with the parents and that he would now keep the children, ending any hope of a peaceful exchange.

In 1992, following another investigation and remarkable achievements in fingerprint technology, authorities identified the author of the letters as a local man who was just a teenager at the time of the hoax. He reportedly wrote and mailed the letters as "a joke."

False Closure

Then, in November 2013, South Australian police received an anonymous tip claiming that the children were buried underneath a warehouse located in North Plympton. Although radar identified "one small anomaly, which can indicate movement or objects within the soil," no evidence was ever found.

The Suspects

Bevan Spencer von Einem

Bevan Spencer von Einem has long been considered the prime suspect in the disappearance of the Beaumont children. Einem was convicted of the July 1983 murder of fifteen-year-old Richard Kelvin, son of a popular news reporter, in 1984. Police have long suspected Einem of working with a series of accomplices and of having committed other abductions and murders.

In 1983, a police informant known as "Mr. B" told police that Einem claimed to have taken three children from a beach to perform medical "experiments," claiming that he performed "brilliant surgery" on the three children before accidentally killing one of them. Following the child's accidental death, the informant stated that Einem claimed to have killed the other two children and buried them in an open field outside the city of Adelaide.

Einem did bare some resemblance to the descriptions of the tall blond man given to police following the disappearance of the Beaumont children and was known to frequent Glenely Beach to spy on people in the changing rooms. He was also noted as having an obsession with children.

Einem worked as an accountant and lived with his mother. There were rumors that he was part of a ring of Adelaide professionals who shared a "hobby" of kidnapping, drugging and raping boys.

"Einem did match the description of the police sketches," Orange said. "And he did like to frequent the same beach. He seemed more interested in young teenage males as his list of known victims would indicate. Einem was a homosexual who picked up hitchhikers with his transvestite friend where they would engage in a "rough trade" style of sex. He would take photographs of his victims as a keepsake. The three young children would seem to be outside of his modus operandi."

However, Einem was significantly younger than the suspect described by witnesses; Einem was around 20 years old at the time, while the description of the suspect placed him in his late 20s. But, in 2007 local police officers identified a young man who looked exactly like a young Einem in Channel 7 news footage of the incident taken days after the disappearance. He remains a prime suspect in the case.

"The newly found news footage does implicate Einem in a psychological way," Orange said. "Killers often like to return to the scene of the crime. He was spotted on film, days after the disappearance. What are the odds against that?"

Arthur Stanley Brown

Arthur Stanley Brown, along with Einem, is considered to be one of two prime suspects in the abduction of the Beaumont children. In 1988, Brown, then 86 years old, was charged with kidnapping, raping, and murdering Judith and Susan Mackey in Townsville, Queensland. His first trial was declared a mistrial after the jury failed to reach a verdict in the case and his second trial was blocked because he was declared unfit to stand trial; Brown was suffering from dementia and Alzheimer's disease by this time.

He is considered one of two prime suspects in the case because of his connection to the murder of other children and because of his remarkable resemblance to descriptions of the tall blond man seen with the children at the time of their disappearance. He was also a prime suspect in the Adelaide Oval case, which involved the disappearance of Joanna Ratcliffe and Kirste Gordon.

"Brown was a known pedophile by his closest family members," Orange said. "He is alleged to have molested numerous younger relatives. He could be placed in the same area and time of the Beaumont children but nothing could be proven."

Although Brown is considered to be a prime suspect in the disappearance of the Beaumont children, the suspect in the case was identified as being in his late 30s; Brown was in his 50s at the time. Brown died in 2002 without ever admitting to the crime.

"Brown would move into a nursing home at the end of his life," Orange said. "He would die an innocent man with the courts never able to officially charge him because of his Alzheimer's."

James Ryan O'Neill

James Ryan O'Neill, convicted of murdering nine-year-old Ricky John Smith in the Australian state of Tasmania in 1975 and currently serving a life sentence for the crime, was considered as a suspect in the Beaumont children disappearance for some time. He is reported as having told several friends in the early 1970s that he was responsible for the disappearance of the Beaumont children in 1966. However, he was publicly eliminated as a suspect by the South Australian police. He remains in prison in Tasmania to this day.

"O'Neill was the subject of a documentary called 'The Fishermen,'" Orange said. "In the documentary, he is evasive about being the man behind the disappearance of the children. He is, however, at the forefront of most pundits who have studied the story. While Brown and Einem did not have charming personas, O'Neill did. He was handsome and smiley with the ability to manipulate everyone around him. He could fabricate lies at the drop of a hat so it is easy to believe that he would be able to charm the children into his acquaintance. People who knew him all described him as 'the most likable man you'll ever meet.' No one could believe that he would be capable of such an act."

Derek Ernest Percy

In 2007, the Victorian newspaper The Age published a report stating that Derek Ernest Percy, at the time the longest-serving prisoner in the southeastern Australian state, was responsible for the disappearance of the Beaumont children in 1966. Initially jailed in 1970 for the 1969 murder of 12-year-old Yvonne Tuohy, Percy was found not guilty of the crime by reason of insanity, but was nonetheless jailed "indefinitely."

He is widely considered to be Australia's worst child serial killer and is suspected of the killings of the Beaumont children, as well as the abduction, attempted rape, and stabbing of Marianne Schmidt and Christine Sharrock on January 11, 1965. In October 2014, Percy was also ruled to have abducted and killed seven-year-old Linda Stilwell in 1968. However, Percy passed away from cancer in 2013, having never admitted to any of his crimes. He remains a possible suspect in the case.

"Percy is unique in that he may have had his mother not aiding him but covering up for him," Orange said. "He is certainly one of the most sadistic pedophiles on record, his doings are unmentionable out of respect for his victims. He was in the city at the time of the Beaumont children disappearance and is probably the top suspect along with O'Neill. His mother, however, has thrown out a lot of what could have been evidence in the case."

Related Cases

Two similar cases to the disappearance of the Beaumont children attracted widespread attention in the South Australian media, and the primary suspect in the Beaumont children's kidnapping case was convicted in one case and suspected in the other.

The Adelaide Oval Case

On August 25, 1972, two young girls, Joanne Ratcliffe (aged 11) and Kirste Gordon (aged 4) went missing while attending an

Australian football game. They are presumed dead. This case also received widespread attention in the South Australian media and Bevan Spencer von Einem was considered the primary suspect in their disappearance.

Einem matched the descriptions of the tall blond man provided by witnesses in the Beaumont children's case and closely resembles the police sketch released to the public. A private police report in leaked in 1989 identified Einem as the primary suspect in the case.

The Family Murders

From 1973 to 1983, a group of men is believed to have been involved in the abduction, rape, and murder of a series of young men and male teenagers in the Adelaide area. Five teens were killed during this time period, including Alan Barnes (aged 16), Neil Muir (aged 25), Peter Stogneff (aged 14), Mark Langley (aged 18), and Richard Kelvin (aged 15). All victims were abducted and subjected to extended bouts of torture and physical assault, including sexual assault and medical experimentation.

Bevan Spencer von Einem was convicted of the abduction and murder of Richard Kelvin 1984 and is currently serving life in prison in Port Augusta prison. In 1990, he was also charged with the murder of Alan Barnes and Mark Langley, but key evidence from the Richard Kelvin murder was ruled inadmissible in the trial. Following the ruling against this key evidence, the prosecution dropped these charges against Einem on December 21, 1990.

Although Einem was the only member of this group to be convicted, and four out of five of The Family Murders remain unsolved, law enforcement officials believe that Einem was part of a white-collar group that preyed on young children. He remains the prime, and only living, suspect in the disappearance of the Beaumont children.

Impact on the Parents

Jim and Nancy Beaumont continued to hold out hope of finding their children for several decades after their disappearance. In fact, the couple continued to live at the Somerton Park home, at 109 Harding Street, that they shared with their children for nearly two decades, hoping that the children would return home someday. Nancy Beaumont was reported as saying that it would be "dreadful" if the children returned to the home only to find that their parents had moved.

"The Beaumonts left the rooms of the children untouched," Orange said. "Every toy, every book even the bed was left exactly as the children had left them."

The couple were never considered as suspects in the case and cooperated with the police at every turn in the investigation, including working with the police and searching in vain every time a new lead developed in the case over the next several decades.

According to The Age, the parents "have since separated, but still live in Adelaide." The stress and sorrow that resulted from their children's abduction, combined with the constant new leads and media attention is said to have contributed to the failure of their marriage.

Jim, in particular, is said to still be suffering from intense and inconsolable grief every time a new development is reported. Nancy was also reported to have suffered extreme grief and horror when, in 1990, several Australian newspapers released computer-generated images of what her children would look like after aging several decades. She reportedly refused to look at the pictures.

"Jim was a little bit stronger than Nancy," Orange said. "He would address the media more than she did. But they both suffered terribly for the rest of their lives into their eighties. They would spend over fifty years wishing for their children's return, getting false hope after false hope, one false lead after another which would all ultimately turn up nothing. It was a horrific cruelty."

Lastly, Jim and Nancy have largely been seen as sympathetic and pitiable figures in the Australian media and in society at large. Although their actions may seem reckless or irresponsible by today's standards, Australian society was viewed as extremely safe in the 1960s and their policy of allowing a child to supervise their younger siblings both in the home and in public was practiced by a large portion of Australian parents.

Impact on Australian Society

The disappearance of the Beaumont children became an overnight sensation in Australia, led to one of the largest police searches in the country's history, and remains the most famous missing persons case in the country. Prior to this incident, Australia was largely viewed as one of the safest societies on the planet and children were allowed to roam freely, doors remained unlocked at all times, and there was little fear of strangers. All of that changed overnight.

"Australia lost its innocence with the disappearance of the Beaumont Children," Orange said. "For three young children to disappear was unheard of. The city where they grew up was a dignified place, a safe place. But it was all an illusion that went away the day the children went missing."

During the initial search for the children, Jim Beaumont went on national television to appeal for their safe return. His heartfelt address to the nation had a lasting impact on the parents and children who watched his plea. Hundreds of viewers called into the station to offer tips and Australian police report that hundreds of tips continue to come in every year to this day. His image on national television continues to serve as a warning for those who believe in the incorruptibility of their fellow citizens and in the safety of their country.

"A lot of people today will blame the parents for letting them go on the bus alone," Adelaide resident Rachel Harding said. "But times were different back then. Back then kids would walk to school by themselves. Kids were told not to talk to strangers. The Beaumonts did tell their children to not talk to children. But child molesters are cunning monsters. My guess is that he may have stolen the eldest child's purse then conned them into seeing him as their benefactor. They would not have had money to get home then along comes this "blonde man" who offers them money. Buys them food and promises to take them home."

Children who came of age in Australia during the 1960s have remarked that there was a definite culture shift following the Beaumont children's disappearance, often describing a "before" and "after." While children were once allowed to roam freely and interact with strangers, Australian parents have since altered their style of parenting and curtailed the amount of freedom offered to young children.

"It was the type of case where we believe there was a lone offender," Australian police detective Des Bray said. "It isn't the type of crime where one would go around bragging about. But we do hope that he told someone and that somebody knows something."

If the Beaumont children are alive today, they would all be in their 50s and would have lived through years of hearing their names and story broadcast on national television and reported on breathlessly in national newspapers. Despite the vast amount of information we have on the case, their fates may never be known with any certainty.

Both Jim and Nancy Beaumont are still alive, and as of this writing they are ninety and eighty-years old respectively. The anonymous tips and false hopes continue to come in today as they did over fifty years ago.